South Park
PERILS

South Park
PERILS
SHORT ROPES & TRUE TALES
OF HISTORIC PARK COUNTY, COLORADO

⚒ Christie Wright ⚒

FILTER PRESS, LLC
Palmer Lake, Colorado

South Park Perils: Short Ropes and True Tales by Christie Wright
ISBN:978-0-86541-152-4
Library of Congress Control Number: 2013944624

Cover "mug shots" are courtesy the Colorado State Archives.
Cover image of Hepburn ranch house is courtesy Park County Local History Archives.
Cover image of John Hoover grave site is courtesy Sean Brubaker, Evoke Images.
Cover image of McLaughlin's Livery is courtesy Park County Local History Archives.
Cover image of the Jefferson depot is courtesy Park County Local History Archives.

BOOK & COVER DESIGN by Robert Schram, Bookends Publication Design

FILTER PRESS LLC

P.O. Box 95 • Palmer Lake, CO 80133
888.570.2663
FilterPressBooks.com
Printed in the United States of America

Dedication

For Becky and Jenny

And for all Colorado's 19th century murder victims

⊰CONTENTS⊱

SECTION FOUR: The Central Towns

SECTION FIVE: The Southern Ranches

Park County map developed by Gary Nichols for the Park County Tourism Department. Used with permission.

⊰INTRODUCTION⊱

Park County, one of the seventeen counties created in 1861 by the first Colorado Territorial legislature, had its own brand of life in the Wild West during its frontier era from 1859 until the turn of the century. The county's unique geography is a contrast of high mountain ranges and low broad plains. Its vast landmass stretches more than 2,000 square miles. These physical features fostered pockets of crime in the outlying areas and human conflicts in the developing towns.

The low-lying area called the South Park Basin is a beautiful expanse of rolling hills and sunken plains created by an inland ocean more than sixty-five million years ago. This is the breathtaking view seen from the top of Kenosha Pass on Highway 285 southeast of Denver and from Wilkerson Pass on Highway 24 northwest of Colorado Springs. Well-known writers, including Walt Whitman, Helen Hunt Jackson, and Samuel Bowles, have penned eloquent descriptions of the South Park scenery.

The South Park Basin was the hunting grounds of American Indians and European fur trappers before 1859, the year Park County's gold rush began. Years earlier, around 1803, a trapper named James Pursley (or Purcell), had found gold at the headwaters of the Platte River. He carried the flakes in his shot-pouch, eventually traveling to Santa Fe, New Mexico, where he was jailed. There he joined explorer Zebulon Pike who was also being held by the Spaniards. Pursley confided to Pike that he did not disclose the source of the gold to his captors. Pike proclaimed him a hero, theorizing that if Pursley had done this, the Spaniards would have rushed to the Rockies and claimed the gold and the land as their own.

Park County's gold rush drew miners to both the north and the west regions of the Colorado Territory. The north drew miners from the Georgia diggings, north of Denver near Black Hawk, who had become disillusioned and traveled south into the park. When one of the miners was killed by Indians, a second group of miners came into the park to hunt for the killers. Along the way, they stopped near the foot of what is now Boreas Pass and panned for gold. The rich creek beds soon yielded up the shiny stuff, and the Hamilton mining camp was formed, with adjoining Tarryall Mining Camp following soon after. The latter was so-named when one of the miners liked the spot so well that he suggested they remain awhile or "tarry all."

The "Pikes Peak or Bust" mining crowd traveled from present-day Colorado Springs up Ute Pass and into western Park County. Gold was discovered in 1859 a few miles west of Alma in what was called the Buckskin Joe mining camp. The Phillips Mine, the first gold mine in the camp, was said to have been discovered when a mountain man named Buckskin Joe fired his gun at a deer but missed. The bullet struck the ore vein, exposing the gold.

The mining towns of Fairplay (1862), Alma (1872), and Como (1879) were established to provide goods and services to miners, ranchers, railroad workers, loggers, and merchandisers. Homestead settlements came in 1862 after the passage of the Homestead Act under President Abraham Lincoln. The town of Guffey was settled much later, in 1896, after Cripple Creek miners came west from the Pikes Peak area to prospect.

Like other new Colorado counties, Park's population included well-meaning settlers as well as the usual variety of "bummers," "no-goods," and "roughs." This jumble of humanity—3,970 folks in 1880—created a mix of positive and negative influences. Given the county's physical size, it was a "fer piece" to travel to fetch help when trouble came calling. Fairplay, designated the county seat in 1867, hosted the only sheriff and a precious few deputies to answer the call to ride to the outlying areas. As a result, problems in the remote areas of the county took second place to the troubles in town that kept the lawmen busy.

If a core sample of early pioneers could have been drilled, it would have shown a good representation of America's melting pot. In the following pages, the reader will meet men with common names—such as David Morris, James Smith, and Frank Jones. Their victims bore names that reflected their heritage, such as Amos Brazille, Martin O'Gorman, and Uplide Vallie. In reading about them, you may discover a pattern: many of the killings were committed during a fit of anger, with much anguish and remorse afterward. Some culprits were caught, tried, and sentenced to prison; others were acquitted, and still others went into hiding, never to be apprehended. Some suspects immediately rode to the nearest town to turn themselves in to a law officer—not because of a sudden awakening of conscience, but to avoid "decorating a tree" at the hands of an angry mob!

Interestingly, there were very few murders that resulted from mining disputes, even though mining was the area's primary industry. The reason may be that mining camps often established their own written laws that spelled out swift penalties for violations. Granted, there was a fair amount of claim-jumping, but Park County had very few murders as a result of mining disputes.

The reader will also meet the ever-faithful sheriffs: Assyria "Cy" Hall, John Ifinger, Daniel H. Wilson, Silas Polluck, and Daniel Kline, among others. A number of the local town marshals are also mentioned, including one who was killed in Como in 1894.

What about women of the time? Three women were charged as accessories to murder; all were acquitted at trial. One woman was killed by her husband on the excuse that she had been nagging him all day. But day to day, women were as prominent a force in the county as the nineteenth century allowed. They often did both woman's work and that of a man. Rancher Marie Guiraud raised nine children and managed her 5,000-acre ranch after her husband died. Sadie Maxey was elected school superintendent in 1894 and reportedly did an outstanding job. Fannie E. Smith mined right alongside the "boys" and didn't hesitate to take her contemporaries to court for the slightest mining infractions. Upon her death, the townsfolk took up a collection to cover her burial expenses in the Buckskin cemetery.

Criminal mayhem and a "spirit of lawlessness" did not permeate all aspects of the early years of Park County. Many cultural activities were enjoyed in the South Park region during Colorado's formative years, including lectures, choir practice, church picnics, Fourth of July parades, school parties, dances, and of course the ever-interesting political debates by "stem-winders." In fact, the approximately fifty known murders in the county over a forty-year period (from 1863 to 1903) boil down to 1.25 murders per year (little consolation, though, to the victims and their families). This time period was chosen because most of the settlement occurred during this time and the fact that primary research sources were plentiful.

In 2009, the South Park National Heritage Area was created to include most of Park County. It is one of only forty-nine areas in the

United States to be so designated by Congress. Then U.S. Senator Ken Salazar, and later Secretary of the Interior, assisted with the nomination and designation. In his 2010 announcement of the bill's passing, Secretary Salazar noted: "The working ranches, clear streams, and frontier stories of South Park are a national treasure that more Americans should have the opportunity to experience."

South Park Perils uniquely gathers the area's true crime frontier stories in one place. Readers will gain insight into the types of law violations, their frequency, and the subsequent legal and social responses at the time—and it provides a simple guide to locating the sites where the crimes were committed.

HOW TO USE THIS BOOK

The stories in this book are organized by the county's geographical regions. Although these regions are varied, they are connected by similar types of crimes and, in some cases, similar land features such as the flat meadows of northern and southern ranches. The book begins at Park County's northernmost end, provides a brief historical overview of the area, and then works down to the southeastern corner.

To visit the historic murder sites, refer to a detailed map of the location. Brief directions at the end of each chapter will give the general location of the setting of the stories. Please be aware that many of the sites are on private property and trespassing is prohibited.

South Park Perils is divided into five sections.

Section One: The Platte Canyon area where railroading, ranching, and timbering prevailed.

Section Two: Fifteen miles west on Highway 285 is the Hall Valley Mining District. Although not large in size, the remote location encouraged quite a bit of illegal activity, earning this area a bad reputation at its onset. A double lynching served to quell the rough going-ons.

Section Three: From Kenosha Pass, the county opens up into a large ranching area, termed the Northern Ranches and the Tarryall Region. The Tarryall Region follows Tarryall Creek on the east side of Highway 285, although Tarryall's original location was on the west side, near Como. A smaller rise, called Red Hill Pass, was the scene of several crimes.

Section Four: The Central Towns. A wild array of shootings and lynchings occurred in the towns of Como, Fairplay, and Alma, along and off of Highway 285.

Section Five: The South Park Basin area, in the middle of the county (and the center of the state); Trout Creek Pass; and the southern ranches on Currant Creek near Guffey.

Within a day's drive, the reader can view several murder locales and scenery that is, according to Frank Hall, "as resplendent a vision viewed from the elevated ranges which wall it in, as the sun ever shone upon."

Please respect private property and do not trespass. Every effort has been made to alert the reader to private property, but ownership and signage change. Again, please be aware and respect 'No Trespassing' signs when exploring.

Enjoy your outlaw journey through historic Park County!

The Platte Canyon

The original stage route from Denver to Park County began in Lakewood near Kipling Avenue and went through Platte Canyon. Winding up through the "hogback" (Turkey Creek Canyon), the route passed several way stations such as the Bergen, Omaha, and Bradford Houses. Ahead lay Slaghts, a stage stop on the Denver-Leadville stage line, near the town of Shawnee, which at one time was called Fairville. Then on to Charles Hepburn's ranch in Long Meadow with its log cabin hotel. From there, the road proceeded on to Webster and Grant, over Kenosha Hill, and down into South Park. An excellent account of the trip by stage through the canyon was printed in an article entitled "Summer Saunterings," in the July 29, 1870, edition of the *Rocky Mountain News*. This was a heavily traveled toll road, called the Denver and South Park Stage Road or Wagon Road.

Farming was popular in this area in the mid-1800s and into the 1900s. The primary crops were lettuce, potatoes, and other root vegetables that could tolerate a short growing season. Lumbering was the main industry, and once construction began on the railroad bed for the Denver, South Park & Pacific Railroad in the 1870s, business increased significantly to provide the railroad ties. There was some mining in the canyon, but none of any significance. After the railroad was established, other industries sprang up, including an ice business run by the Maddox family from 1903 through 1937, and trout fishing for vacationers, often advertised in railroad brochures and tourist magazines. The train stopped on its way to Leadville and let fishermen out for the day, picking them up at the same place on the return route in the evening.

Today, the canyon is home to the towns of Pine, Bailey, Shawnee, Grant, and Webster and is still a tourist destination.

This scenic spot on the North Fork Ranch might be the site of Oliver Callahan's murder. The exact location of the shooting is unknown, and all of the North Fork Ranch is private property. *Courtesy Christie Wright*

Chapter One

MURDER at the RICEVILLE SWITCH
1896

I n June 1878, the narrow gauge track of the Denver, South Park
& Pacific Railroad reached Platte Canyon, providing a vital
transportation line into Park County. Brief stopping areas or
switches along the way allowed local ranchers to load their hay,
dairy products, or produce for shipping. Riceville had a seven-car
siding for this very purpose. A railroad siding is a short track spur
where trains could temporarily park unused boxcars or use the
track to go around another train.

Brothers Harvey Hubert Rice and John Henry Rice were two of the
ranchers who used the Riceville siding. They married daughters of Ben
Tyler, an early homesteader in the canyon. Harvey married Alice Tyler
in 1924, and John wed Ella Marie Tyler in 1927. The Rice brothers' property was located between Shawnee and Long Meadow and the siding
was soon dubbed the Riceville Switch. Several cabins on the ranch
were built by Raymond Knisely, who lived nearby with his family.

On December 24, 1896, Oliver Callahan, a well-respected lumberman who ran a tie camp near the Riceville Switch, was at work when
an acquaintance shot and killed him. The reason? A loan Callahan
had made to Oscar Stringham, one of his employees, for a team of
horses. Word had circulated that Stringham planned to sell the team
even though Callahan still held the note on the horses. Callahan had
operated his mill in the area for approximately one year and was
well-liked by his employees. He had even helped Stringham and his
family with food and other necessities when they fell on hard times.

Around nine the morning of Christmas Eve, Callahan got wind
that Stringham was planning to sell the horses. He proceeded at

once to Stringham's house to discuss the matter. Stringham was
hiding in the bushes waiting to ambush his boss. As Callahan passed
him, Stringham shot him. Grabbing his chest, the victim shouted,
"Oh my God boys, I am shot!" then fell, mortally wounded.

Stringham dashed into the nearby hills. As he fled, he shouted
out a three-word confession to a co-worker named Elmer Chase:
"I've killed Callahan!"

Stringham watched from atop the canyon bluffs to see if
Callahan was actually dead; when it appeared so, he took off for
Denver on the train. Twenty men soon assembled to pursue the
killer, but they came up empty-handed.

A man matching Oscar Stringham's description was seen on the
South Park train pulling into Denver that evening. The suspicious
fellow had two ill-concealed pistols, one in each hip pocket. Although
mounted officers searched the area, the man seen on the train was
nowhere to be found. A brief false alarm stirred up some excitement in
the city on Christmas night, when a man with similar looks was found
lying drunk on Denver's Market Street. He turned out to be an escapee
from the Denver County jail, where he was returned to sleep it off.

Sheriff Daniel H. Wilson made the thirty-five mile trip from
Fairplay to Riceville on Christmas Eve and spent the entire afternoon scouring the foothills for the killer. Wilson then sent
Stringham's description to nearby law enforcement authorities, in
hopes they would recognize and arrest him. Stringham, meanwhile,
made his way from Denver north to Greeley, Colorado, where he
stayed for a few weeks with his father-in-law.

Coroner Dr. O. J. Mayne arrived from Como on Christmas Eve
to hold the inquest at Riceville. Oddly, Mrs. Stringham appeared at
the proceedings. "Much hard feeling was manifested against her,"
the *Rocky Mountain News* noted on December 26, 1896.

The Park County Commissioners asked Governor Albert
McIntyre to issue a reward for Stringham's apprehension, which he
did. To help the public recognize the killer the *Rocky Mountain
News* of December 26, 1896, described the wanted man this way:

> Oscar Stringham is about 35 years of age, about 6 feet 0 inches in
> height, dark complexion, hair and mustache, had a small face and
> chin whiskers. He had a particularly sneakish look, which had

been commented upon at the lumber camp more than once.

A second description was printed in the same paper four days later:

He is described as follows: Dark hair, one-half gray, very curly; smooth teeth, two upper front teeth longer than the rest; high cheek bones; short face, regular bulldog jaw; dish-faced; resembles Cherokee Indian; weight 120 pounds, height 5 feet 4 inches, moustache and chin whiskers, first finger on right hand larger at second joint and tapers to a point.

To add to the intrigue, a second suspect emerged the day after Christmas: the husband of Callahan's housekeeper, a Mr. Van Camp. He was suspected of threatening Callahan after Mrs. Van Camp left her husband in Denver to take the domestic position in Riceville. Supposedly, the enraged man wrote two letters to Callahan, threatening his life if he did not discharge his wife from her duties. This rumor promptly blew over, however, and nothing more came of it.

At his father-in-law's urging, Oscar Stringham turned himself in to Weld County Sheriff Clark on January 14, 1897. Sheriffs Clark and Wilson rendezvoused in Denver the following night, the exchange was made, and Wilson escorted his prisoner back to Fairplay's stone jail.

On February 9, 1897, Stringham was taken back to the Riceville area to appear before Justice of the Peace J. H. McDonald for a preliminary hearing. He was held without bond, and his trial date was set for the May 1898 term of District Court.

Surprisingly, Stringham was acquitted. His attorney successfully pleaded self-defense. Despite his confession to Elmer Chase, Stringham was a free man. Chase heard the shots and heard Stringham's shouted confession, but he did not see the actual shooting. No eyewitnesses, no conviction. Such was the law near the turn of the century.

THE RICEVILLE SITE TODAY

The Riceville Switch is now a popular dude ranch and fishing lodge called the North Fork Ranch, accessed at mile marker 218 on the north side of Highway 285, a few miles south of Shawnee. The ranch is accredited by Orvis and is a delightful place to stay for a week.

Permission from the owners is required to drive on the ranch grounds.

The Hepburn's ranch house that Paisley and Daniel Wetzel, aka Mudd, ransacked after tying Charles Hepburn up in his barn. The structure is no longer standing. *Courtesy Park County Local History Archives #2223. Source: Hal Ostertag Family.*

Chapter Two

A PIONEER PUMMELED
1898

Charles Hepburn and his cousin Edwin were true "pioneers of the Park," coming to the Colorado Territory in the early 1860s from Colton, New York. They initially settled in the town of Montgomery, at the foot of Mount Lincoln, during the first gold and silver boom. Edwin became the Montgomery Mining District's clerk and recorder. Charles was part owner of a hotel there but later sold his portion through his friend, Wilbur F. Stone.

In 1865, Charles Hepburn and a new partner, Mr. Brock, took out a liquor license for the Kenosha House, a busy hotel near the top of Kenosha Pass. They soon moved a few miles east to the 76 Ranch, where they set up a hotel in a log cabin and also farmed a large potato field. On November 3, 1867, Charles married Agnes D. Wood, who was from his hometown in New York. Returning to Platte Canyon, the couple remained at the ranch as managers and continued farming. Agnes was his constant companion, fondly referring to her husband as "C.L." Although adjusting to the West's openness and isolation was difficult for her, she became an avid fisherwoman but detailed her loneliness in a daily diary.

Eventually, the pioneering couple moved to an adjoining ranch, Long Meadow, where they continued living for many years. The Hepburns also ran a post office for a number of years. Once the railroad arrived in the canyon in 1879, Long Meadow had its own siding.

Life in Platte Canyon was peaceful and pleasant in the Hepburns' later years, until late afternoon on February 17, 1898. Charles Hepburn, age eighty-two, went about his usual evening

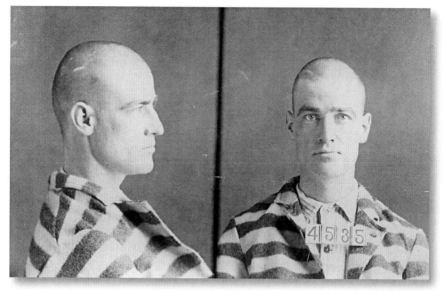

Charles Paisley's mug shot after he was issued the standard striped uniform and had his head shaved. *Courtesy Colorado State Archives*

chores in the chilly barn when suddenly two men, William Paisley and Daniel Wetzel (aka Daniel Mudd), accosted him, threw a sack over his head, and threatened, "Damn you, keep quiet or we will kill you!"

The robbers assaulted the elderly gentleman to the point of unconsciousness. After binding his hands and feet with rope and strips of sack, they dragged his limp body into a barn stall, covered it with straw, and laid in wait for Mrs. Hepburn to come check on her husband.

When Agnes entered the barn, Paisley and Wetzel snuck out and dashed to the ranch house, ransacking it in search of money. The two hightailed it to Denver, where Paisley was captured on Larimer Street a few days later. Wetzel took off for parts unknown, and although the county offered a twenty-five dollar reward for his capture, there is no evidence he was ever caught or brought to trial in Colorado.

Paisley had his day in court on May 20, 1898, and was sentenced to fourteen years in prison. The amount of money he stole from the house was all of one dollar and forty-five cents. Charles Hepburn died eight months later from his injuries. Agnes succumbed to a lingering illness seven years later.

The Hepburns are buried in the White Cemetery at the foot of Kenosha Pass on the east side.

LONG MEADOW RANCH TODAY

The old Hepburn ranch is still intact, although the original buildings were replaced years ago. It is just past mile marker 220 on Highway 285; a wooden sign reading "Long Meadow" above the gravel driveway marks the entrance. This is private property—do not enter! A pullout on the highway just before the sign allows a nice view of Long Meadow. The ranch retains its historic appearance, helping the reader to picture two men with kerchiefs covering their faces galloping away in late afternoon February 17, 1898.

Death of C. L. Hepburn.

Mr. C. L. Hepburn died at his ranch in Platte cañon the 3d inst. He was nearly 81 years of age, which had a great deal to do with his death, although it is said he never recovered from the beating he received by the two robbers last February.

Mr. Hepburn was one of the oldest of old-timers in Park county, having settled on his ranch in the early sixties, where he has lived an honored and respected citizen against whose uprightness and character no breath has ever been whispered. He leaves a widow to mourn his departure. The funeral at Chase was largely attended by the cañon people.

Charles Hepburn's obituary as printed in the *Fairplay Flume*, October 14, 1898.

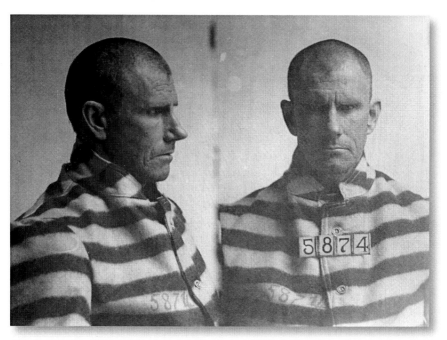

Charles Combs, inmate # 5874, presents a formidable appearance. He was received at the Colorado State Prison on October 25, 1903, *Courtesy Colorado State Archives*

Chapter Three

ONE MAN, TWO SHOOTINGS
1903

Eight miles west of Long Meadow, in the small town of Grant, Charles P. Combs owned a saloon off and on for fifteen years. The *Denver Post* on December 1, 1902, described him as well-to-do, noting he was a deputy sheriff in those parts. Before coming to Grant, Charley Combs was in the liquor business in Mosquito Gulch, one of the important mining camps south of Fairplay. He was also present when two men gunned down saloon owner Pete Cox in Puma City in 1897. (See Chapter 15).

On February 11, 1902, two patrons named McDrake and Charles Madherst came into Combs's bar around 5 o'clock, at the end of their work shift; both were already feeling no pain. McDrake picked a quarrel with Combs and grabbed Madherst's large Bowie knife. Pointing it at Combs, he ran the owner back behind the bar. Madherst stepped in and overpowered his buddy, relieving him of the weapon before any damage was done. McDrake left the saloon, and Combs's friend James J. (J. J.) Smith secured the knife—an ironic twist, given that Smith had shot and killed his neighbor John Grow seventeen years earlier, in 1885, over a cattle boundary dispute (See Chapter 11).

McDrake returned to the saloon at 7:30 p.m., threw back a couple more drinks, and overheard Madherst making threats outside. McDrake pulled out his own pocket knife and started for the door. Smith and Combs told him not to go out with the knife, but McDrake insisted. Combs tried to stop him, whereupon McDrake struck at the saloon owner with the small knife, almost cutting him. He followed Combs back to the bar, where the saloon keeper grabbed a hidden revolver.

Smith told Combs, "Keep your cool and don't shoot unless you have to." But within seconds, Combs decided the need had arisen, and he fired. McDrake fell to the floor with a bullet wound to the lung.

McDrake was taken to a Denver County hospital with severe injuries, but he eventually recovered. Upon his discharge from the hospital, he swore vengeance on his assailant that promised to be "as bitter as any of the fatal affrays in the Kentucky mountains," according to a *Denver Post* article on December 1, 1902. He also had the hospital send the bill to Combs, claiming the latter agreed to pay it, which was not true; Combs adamantly refused to cover the charges.

Around November 1, 1902, Combs received a letter postmarked from Denver, ordering him out of the county and threatening that unless he left, he would be killed no matter where he was and his "other property" would be burned. The anonymous writer gave him until November 10, 1902, to vacate or else.

November 10 passed with no threats or assaults, although many Grant residents took the warning to mean their entire town would be burned. Men were constantly on the lookout and carried weapons while traveling. Combs, too, was always armed. He painted the interior windows of his business so no one could peer inside to see if he was in the saloon. He did not want to be an easy target. He told the *Denver Post* on December 1, 1902:

> "I'm ready for them, let them come.". . . He has his rifle at his side, his home is guarded and he wears a revolver in handy fashion. He is a large powerful man, weighing nearly two hundred pounds, and has the reputation of being a good marksman.

All was quiet for the month of November—almost. After enjoying Thanksgiving with his family, Charley Combs and several cronies played cards in his saloon that evening. The men sat near the north window, their forms illuminated by a lamp that cast their shadows. The angle at which they were seated projected a shadow four inches to the side and not straight on. Suddenly, three shots in rapid succession whizzed through the window and into the bar. The intended targets had no time to move. They sat frozen in their seats, mouths open, staring at each other. All was silent.

One of the friends noticed blood oozing from Charley's head and sent for a doctor. After cleaning the wound, the doctor discovered it had come from a piece of flying glass and said Charley would be no worse for the wear. An alert was put out to find McDrake, but he was not tracked down.

An incident fifteen months after this scare proved to be Combs's undoing. In May 1903, once again in his saloon, Combs was involved in a much more personal and tragic shooting. He reported that his wife, Mattie, had been coming into the saloon throughout the day, badgering him. Toward evening, he was fed up and heard her talking as he sat with his back to her. Cocking his revolver, he spun around and fired indiscriminately, hoping to scare her away. Instead, the bullet struck her in the chest and exited her back.

Combs carried his wife into the house and tended to her the rest of the night, and she appeared to be fine. He telegraphed for Dr. Mayne to come from Como, and he arrived the next morning via train. He treated the wound as best he could, but advised that she go to a hospital in Denver. Mattie Combs succumbed to her injuries in a Denver hospital three days later on May 29, 1903, and was laid to rest at Fairmont Cemetery. The couple had been married only four years.

A warrant was issued for Combs's arrest. Sheriff Silas Pollock proceeded to Grant on May 31 to arrest the penitent husband and bring him back to Fairplay to file charges. But Combs had sold the saloon and fixtures to another Grant resident, James A. Lamping, and had left town.

He first fled to Denver, then continued north to Grand County, where he found work on the Moffat Road, the railroad line over Rollins Pass—until he recognized a new hire as an old acquaintance from Grant. Combs immediately headed back to Denver to avoid detection, but was recognized and arrested on August 3, 1903, at the Palmer House, a boardinghouse at Sixteenth and Larimer Streets.

Two days later, Combs was in the Park County jail. He trumped up a story for the newspapers, claiming he was shooting his revolver in his yard in Grant when a stray bullet somehow wandered through the window, striking his wife.

On October 23, 1903, a jury decided he was guilty of second-degree murder, and he was ordered to serve from ten to eleven

years in the penitentiary. Sheriff Pollock left for the Canon City
facility with his charge on November 1, and it appears that Charles
P. Combs, inmate #5874, served his full term.

THE MURDER SITE TODAY

Although the town of Grant still stands today, Combs's saloon
is gone. Grant is now the terminus of the road going over Guanella
Pass that dead-ends in Georgetown. The road is a gravel car road
that is paved on one side.

Chapter Four

A FAMILY TRAGEDY: SUICIDE or MURDER?—1899

I n the summer of 1899, a family from Byers, Colorado, moved to Grant. Walter Banes, age thirty-three, was a strapping young man of two hundred pounds, with a broad chest and pleasant smile. He was an up-and-coming teamster, with a fine team of horses, and although not rich by any means, he was doing well and supporting his wife, Jennie, and their two-year-old son. Walter's father, John, and his uncle lived nearby on Comanche Creek, fifteen miles from Grant.

Walter rented the Grant schoolhouse temporarily, until the next school session began on December 4, 1899. In the county's ranching towns, school was typically held only in the winter months, December through mid-March, allowing the children to help their families with the ranch work during the other seasons.

On September 15, 1899, neighbors noticed there was no activity at the schoolhouse. When Phoebe Buno (sometimes spelled "Bruno") went to return a carton of eggs, no one answered the door. Standing on her tiptoes, she peered into the window to see a strange sight: the family was in bed with the sheets pulled up to their necks. Suspecting the worst, she hastened to tell two well-known residents, J. H. McFarland and Harry Provost, who quickly responded and forced the door open. There they discovered a ghastly sight—the family was dead.

The little house was spotless and orderly. There was no sign of forced entry or a scuffle. The *Fairplay Flume* of September 22, 1899, carried this touching description:

AN ENTIRE FAMILY DIES

Mysterious Death of Walter Banes, His Wife and Child in a Mountain Village--Murder or Suicide?--Ghastly Discovery by Neighbors.

Headline from the *Denver Evening Post*, September 16, 1899.

Mrs. Banes lay upon her back, her hands folded across her breast; her mouth, however, was open, which may or may not have been natural. The baby lay partly on his side with his back towards her, one arm somewhat under his father, who lay on the side of the bed farthest from the wall, his left hand over his breast under cover and the right where it would naturally have fallen.

The only suspicious item was a little tin cup containing a small amount of laudanum on a school desk next to the bed that served as their nightstand.

Laudanum was an opium-based concoction mixed with alcohol in liquid form, popular at the time and very addictive.

The crime horrified the locals. It had been three years since rancher Benjamin Ratcliff had wreaked his havoc up on the Tarryall, shooting three school board members at once, also in a school house, the Michigan Creek School. Ratcliff paid for his crime with his life and left a scary aftermath. Not since the "Reign of Terror by the 'Bloody Espinosas,'" who killed six people in Park County in the early 1860s, had such heinous deaths occurred.

Since there were no authorities in Grant to take charge of the remains, residents took turns watching over the bodies, and the tin cup was preserved for later chemical examination. County Coroner

Dr. William Moulton arrived from Alma to initiate the required inquest, impaneling a six-man jury consisting of Orson Bruno (Phoebe's husband), H. White, Henry W. Prevo, David Rasty, A. Tracy, and Henry T. Wattles, foreman. The jury returned a verdict of suicide on September 16, 1899. The coroner's original records have been preserved, which state:

> The above parties met death at their own hands, probably from an overdose of some poisonous drug, the cause being despondency over financial affairs brought about by failing health. The above persons met their death in their own home at Grant of the night of the 14th.

Juror Henry Prevo had testified that Walter Banes had seemed downcast during the last few days when speaking of his past. He told Prevo that he lost his crops at his previous location and was forced to sell his farm outside of Denver.

John Banes was beside himself. He could not believe his son would take his family's life and then his own. He described an excellent relationship between the couple. In addition, $126 was found in a trunk in the school building, which proved that Walter had some savings and that he was not desperate over his finances. Another $100 was found on Walter himself, which was used for funeral expenses.

John Banes scrutinized the scene for the minutest of clues and found a tear in the mosquito netting on one of the windows. Seizing upon this, he explained his theory to the *Denver Post* on September 18, 1899:

> While at the house where my son and his family were murdered and while the coroner's investigation was in progress, I noticed something that they seemed to have overlooked. It is a small thing, but very significant to my mind. The mosquito netting over one of the windows was torn and it had only latterly been pulled down. My theory is that someone chloroformed the family to get their money.

At Banes's request, the bodies were taken to Denver for an autopsy. The *Denver Evening Post* portrayed the procedure in graphic detail. The stomach contents yielded no evidence of poisoning. The suspected method of death was indeed chloroform,

All that is left of the schoolhouse where the Banes family died is the outline of the cement foundation. *Courtesy Christie Wright*

"taken as a gas by breathing," since there was no evidence the family had ingested it or any other toxin. Drinking chloroform would have resulted in a very painful death. Regarding the laudanum, the attending doctor pronounced that the amount found was not enough to cause death and leave the family in such peaceful repose.

Newspapers ran wild theories about the deaths. Some wrote it was a mass suicide, while others were convinced the family members were victims of a triple homicide. The plot thickened when it was learned that Walter was acquainted with a sheepherder in Byers named Otto Goette (aka Brown), who had recently been murdered. Did the young father and his family leave their hometown to escape that man's killer, only to be tracked down?

Goette's story was sensational in its own right. He had disappeared in September 1899 from his Byers ranch, where he had lived for twelve years. His body was found the following spring in a ravine on his property by his neighbor; his skull had been crushed.

His herd of sheep, worth $4,000, had been sold in Omaha, Nebraska, before the crime was discovered. Then in July 1899, another rancher from the same area, Bruno Faber, went missing in Denver. No firm connection was ever made between these deaths and the Banes family, nor were suspects ever located.

While all this was going on, John Banes's wife, Sarah, died two months after their son's death from rheumatism and typhoid fever. Now only one daughter, Cora Banes Gerrard, remained in his family. The Banes were buried in the Fairmont Cemetery in Denver. The definitive cause of the Banes's deaths has never been determined.

THE SCHOOL SITE TODAY

Grant is a small town located at the intersection of Highway 285 and Guanella Pass Road, CR 62. The foundation of the Grant school can be seen in a field approaching Grant from the east. It sits on private property. Please do not trespass.

An historical photograph of the train station in Grant that stood near Reed and Goodwin's bunkhouse. *Courtesy Park County Local History Archives*

Chapter Five

RIDDLED BY REED
1887

Platte Canyon's excellent timber drew extensive lumbering operations to the area from the late 1800s through the 1930s. After the South Park train came through in the late 1870s, "tie camps" were in operation all up and down the valley to provide timbers for the railroad's construction. On February 27, 1879, the *Fairplay Flume* noted the railroad needed fifty thousand cross-ties to lay track over Kenosha Pass. Tie camp workers were called tie-hacks, and sawmill workers were "mill hands" or "lumbermen." George Law owned a sawmill located a quarter mile from the mouth of Geneva Gulch.

On the evening of September 26, 1887, a worker named Charles Reed shot and killed a local teamster named Fred Wallingbury (also spelled Wallingsburg), fulfilling a vow he had made on numerous occasions. His pal Charley Goodwin was charged as an accomplice. Unraveling the story has proved difficult because of the manner in which the eyewitness accounts were written in the coroner's report: incomplete sentences, references to both Goodwin and Reed as "Charley," and statements by a whole lot of people who claimed they "didn't know nothin'" about the shooting.

The county coroner was not available to travel from Fairplay to Grant on the night of the murder. In his absence, local Justice of the Peace J. L. McDonald convened a coroner's panel of six citizens to determine the manner of death. The panel determined that the victim had been shot with "felonious intent." Meanwhile, according to the *Rocky Mountain News* of September 26, 1887, Wallingbury's body was left lying in the road until the panel was convened.

Several witnesses testified before the coroner's panel. Reed did not testify, but Goodwin testified several times and did not hesitate to implicate his partner.

Goodwin testified that he and Reed were bunkmates at the Grant station, one of the railroad stops in Platte Canyon. On the morning of the shooting, Goodwin noticed that Reed was in possession of two guns and had said to him: "Two guns are too many for you. Give me one."

Reed also borrowed a knife belonging to George Williams, another bunkmate, telling him, "I will kill one, two, or three sons-of-bitches in this town before night." Reed appeared to be amassing an arsenal and was gunning for a fight. Reed also told Goodwin and several others that he would kill Fred Wallingbury, that "no good son-of-a-bitch," before he (Fred) left town. No reason was given, other than Wallingbury was known to be "quarrelsome" when drinking, and Reed expressed a fear of being "pounded" by Fred.

Around 6 p.m., Wallingbury started back to the mill from Grant accompanied only by his Ballard rifle slung over his shoulder. Goodwin and Reed first went to the stables and then to the Grant store, where suddenly, Goodwin noticed his partner was missing. Unbeknownst to him and Wallingbury, Reed had started up Geneva Gulch in search of Fred, with one of his guns strapped on.

Goodwin immediately suspected trouble and snagged acquaintance James Coffey to "take a walk" with him. Goodwin confided to Coffey that he was worried Reed might do harm to Wallingbury. They went as far as a barn on the outskirts of town.

"Let's go farther," urged Goodwin. The two set out for Geneva Gulch, when they heard a gunshot about 150 yards ahead. They had proceeded another 30 feet when Reed came running at them, breathless, gun in hand.

"I've done the son-of a bitch," he yelled.

"What have you done?" gasped Goodwin.

"I've shot Wallingbury," shouted Reed. "I've killed that damn Fred, and he's not the first."

"I believe he has done it," said Goodwin, turning to Coffey. "We will go down to town and report it."

Reed then handed Goodwin his gun and grabbed Goodwin's smaller revolver in a quick exchange. Coffey described the shooter's original weapon as "a long gun, about 15 inches long."

"I don't want this gun," Goodwin protested. "Before they get me, I'll use every load in my gun," Reed swore and ran on.

Coffey, Goodwin, and two other men described as "Swedes," who had come upon the scene, walked to the shooting site along with a man named C. Deringer. Sure enough, they found Wallingbury lying dead.

The outcome of the case is unknown, since the *Flume* issues for 1889, which would have reported on the spring term of District Court, are missing. The Denver papers did not carry the story other than the initial *Rocky Mountain News* article entitled "Riddled by Reed." The correspondent opined, "There are no officers here and he will have a good start," implying that Reed would go on the run. Other Platte Canyon suspects certainly had in the past and would in the future.

THE MURDER SITE TODAY

The road up Geneva Gulch is a maintained gravel road. From the town of Grant, drive north on County Road 62 (Guanella Pass Road). There is a pullout wide enough to accommodate a vehicle about one-quarter of a mile from the intersection. The property on both sides of the road is private and trespassing is prohibited.

Grant circa 1900, approximately twenty-four years after McLaine killed John Kane in the area. *Courtesy Park County Local History Archives. Source: Kenn Hicks*

Chapter Six

A BAD COMBINATION in GRANT
1875

Located three miles east of Hall Valley, Geneva Gulch, with Geneva Creek running through, is now the Guanella Pass Road (CR 62), which terminates in Georgetown in Clear Creek County. The route is an enjoyable car ride in the summertime, the scenery is picturesque in the fall, and the area is loaded with history. The old Geneva City site still has run-down cabins and nearby mines. Some of the better producing mines were the Revenue, Silver Queen, and the Josephine. Vast high meadows flatten out and are home to herds of cattle that roam there in the summertime. All this and with the Continental Divide as a backdrop, Geneva is visually a truly spectacular place.

In the 1880s, when mining was booming, men from all walks of life came into the valley to work for $2.50 a day. Isaac McLaine (or McCain), originally from Scotland, was one such fellow. He was twenty-six, fond of whiskey, and fonder yet of shooting up the town when he had had his fill. Described as a "drunken desperado," the miner literally tore up a Grant hotel in the summer of 1875. The June 9, 1876, *Rocky Mountain News* issue described the fiasco as follows:

> He entered the hotel at Grant, drove the people out at the point of his pistol, broke down the doors and smashed all the windows, and held undisputed and unmolested possession of the premises until his whiskey gave out and he vacated at his own sweet pleasure.

This set the backdrop for his next shoot-'em-up on June 3, 1876, once again in a Grant hotel.

John Kane also mined in Geneva Gulch, although it is unknown if the two men worked together. An argument arose between the two inside a hotel, and McLaine shot at Kane but missed. McLaine fired again as Kane ran outside, felling the miner with a single bullet that passed through his right lung, killing him instantly.

Mayhem ensued. McLaine leaped onto his saddled horse and took off at a gallop. Four men, outraged by the senseless shooting, rode after the murderer at full gallop, with guns a-blazing. The makeshift posse was so desperate to stop the killer that they shot his horse right out from under him. Trapped, McLaine threw down his pistol and was escorted to the Fairplay for a little "iron bar therapy."

In the fall of 1876, McLaine was tried and found guilty of murder. He received a life sentence, of which he served twelve years. His sentence was then commuted to twenty-one years, essentially allowing his release from prison.

His pardon by Governor Adams was reprinted in the *Rocky Mountain News*, February 19, 1888.

> The good conduct, feeble health and age of Isaac McLain [sic] have induced the board of penitentiary commissioners and the warden to ask for a pardon for him. I herewith grant their request to the extent of commuting the sentence of Isaac McLain to a term of twenty-one years. Yours truly, ALVA ADAMS, Governor.

McLaine's trail grows cold thereafter.

THE MURDER SITE TODAY

Grant is a small town located at the intersection of Highway 285 and Guanella Pass Road (CR 62).The population dwindled quickly once the railroad stopped running in 1937, but a few buildings remain. The town was named for President Ulysses S. Grant.

Jay and Hattie Draughn with their children. After surviving gunshot wounds in Colorado, Jay was gunned down in 1913 by an inebriated acquaintance on the streets of Hazard, Kentucky. *Courtesy Daniel J. Miller*

Chapter Seven

KENTUCKY BLOOD
SPILLED in COLORADO—1897

Although Kentucky and Colorado are more than 1,200 miles apart, two Kentucky relatives bridged the distance through bloodshed in 1897.

Eastern Kentucky, notorious for fatal family feuds, was the Hatfield's home of "Hatfields and McCoys" infamy. Kentucky was also the seat of other sensational, less publicized, family wars. One involved "Dolph" Draughn and the Devil John Wright gang in Lechner and Knott Counties.

Dolph was deputy sheriff in Knott County in 1885. He had a personal enemy in Washington "Wash" Craft, a member of Devil John Wright's gang, who had killed a friend of Dolph's named Linville Higgins. Dolph himself had murdered a man named Press Day a few years earlier in retaliation for Day killing Dolph's friend, Linville Higgins. Dolph wanted revenge as well as the reward money for Higgins' murder, so he rode into neighboring Letcher County, Kentucky, with a posse to capture Craft. The Wright bunch was laying in wait for him and his posse and they were quickly ambushed. Dolph lost at least one man and his own horse was shot out from under him.

Six years later, in 1891, Dolph decided he needed to get out of Kentucky as did his twenty-three year-old nephew, Rory "Jay" Draughn, who killed Benjamin Cunningham in March 1891 after arguing over a woman at Cunningham's party. Jay was considered a "bad man" in his younger days with a string of bad deeds to prove it.

Uncle and nephew traveled west together, with Dolph using the alias John Caudell (or Codell), while Jay Draughn became Hiram

Dolph Draughn's full name was Alvis Rudolphus Alfonse Lafayette Draughn.
*Courtesy Tony Adkins, from the collection of Emma Alverti Draughn Goodpaster,
daughter of Dolph Draughn.*

Baker, taking his wife's maiden name. Eventually the two landed in
Grant, Colorado, where Jay ran a small sawmill on Geneva Creek,
seven miles from Grant and employed his uncle. Jay's wife, Hattie,
and their three young children traveled out to Colorado join him.

Dolph was irritated with his nephew because Jay had not paid
him $175 in owed wages. Frustrated with each other, the two began
drinking in a Grant saloon on August 18, 1897. When it was time to
go home, the men hitched up the wagon and friends of Hattie
Draughn who were in the area, Mrs. Emma Carthcart and Mrs. Mary
Sullivan, hopped in the wagon to go pay her a visit.

As the team plodded up the roadbed that runs parallel to
Geneva Creek, Dolph became irascible and vulgar with the help of
frequent swigs from a liquor bottle stuck in his pocket. He badgered
the women to drink with him. Concerned for the women's delicate
ears, Jay spoke up and said: "Let us get out and walk, John and let
the ladies drive."

Both men disembarked and started up the steep hill but Jay, the younger and less inebriated of the two, beat his uncle to the top, where Jay's house was located. Straggling up the hill, Dolph finally arrived at the top and snuck up on a nearby resident, John P. Boyer, who was tending a fire at his cabin next to the Baker's.

"Hello John," Dolph called out from about forty feet away. Startled, Boyer looked up to see Dolph's rifle aimed right at him, cocked and ready to fire.

Boyer threw himself backwards and, scrambling quickly, managed to get out of close range of the gun barrel. He then crawled inside his cabin, watching while Dolph approached, weapon still pointed. When Dolph lurched around the corner, Boyer deftly grabbed the barrel with his left hand and the big man's shoulder with his right.

"Oh, I don't intent to shoot you," said Dolph matter-of-factly, offering the shaking man his whiskey bottle. Boyer accepted in hopes it would calm Dolph; however, his opponent's next statement was ominous: "There are some people in the county that do not know me but will know me tonight, for I am going to make a clean sweep." After this, Boyer had a feeling something bad would happen, and he was right.

As the family, including the children and Hattie's friends, sat down to dinner, Dolph suddenly swung the door open and staggered into the dining room, swearing because he had been left behind. He took a seat next to Mary Sullivan, placing his rifle across his knees. Jay informed him, "I will have no such language used in this house! Please step outside, as there are ladies present."

Dolph refused to go and, "with an oath, raised his gun. Mr. Baker (Jay) started for the storeroom door, apparently with the desire to get Caudell (Dolph) from our presence that we should hear nothing further." Dolph then fired at Jay, hitting him in the shoulder. As Jay fell to the floor, he managed to squeeze off a round from his pistol, striking his uncle in the abdomen. One newspaper claimed that as Jay prepared to fire a second shot, his little boy stood in front of him, preventing it. Dolph dropped his rifle into the hands of Mrs. Sullivan and staggered out the back door just as neighbor Boyer came running up, suspecting the worst.

"No use boy, we will both be dead," Dolph groaned to Boyer as he clutched his gut with both hands. The wounded man ran fifty yards to the bunkhouse and collapsed, never to get up again. The Kentucky ex-deputy died the next afternoon. "Caudell never ceased screaming while I remember. I think he died drunk," according to a letter written by witness Mary Sullivan, whose version is quite dramatic. Although in shock, she claimed she ordered Dolph to give her the gun, jumped up, got the rifle and hid it as he staggered outside. She then ran into the next room where Hattie was trying to hold her husband up.

> He fell bleeding to the floor, utterly unconscious. The fore-
> man of the mill jumped on a horse to go for the Dr. but
> I called to him to come back and help get Jay to the bed
> where he lay seeming unconscious, his wife and children
> all screaming at the same time.

Jay eventually made it to the Fairplay Hospital where he was treated for a shattered shoulder and cut right lung. Newspapers carried flashy headlines about the to-do, such as a "Complicated Tale of Blood" and "The Dark Career of a Kentuckian."

Once the true identities of the men were discovered, word reached their home state where Dolph's oldest son, John A. Draughn, vowed revenge on his cousin Jay, for killing John's father. John and Jay had a secondary relationship—that of brother-in-laws: they had married sisters. Because the Park County Coroner's inquest panel had absolved Jay of murder by ruling the killing "self-defense," Jay would not face any legal charges in Colorado. However, John A. knew all about his cousin's deadly antics back home and immediately planned a trip west to bring his wayward cousin to justice in Kentucky for the 1891 killing of Ben Cunningham. Besides, there was a $350 reward on Jay's head for his capture and arrest, and Jay was in no shape to resist.

John's first order of business upon arriving in Denver was a legal quest to find out if Colorado would honor Kentucky's requisition, a formal request from one governor to another. If Colorado Governor Alva Adams would agree to accept the request, the next step would be to ask for an extradition, or fugitive, warrant, allowing John to escort his wayward relative back to Kentucky for prosecution. When he strode up to the new state capitol building on September 10, 1897, the clerks inside could see John was a man on a mission.

"Can I see the governor a minute?" asked John. He was shown into the governor's office at once.

"I want to see if you will honor a requisition from the governor of Kentucky," he announced to Governor Adams. Adams agreed that once an official law enforcement man arrived from Kentucky and took legal custody of Jay, John could accompany them back home.

Next, John boarded the Denver, South Park & Pacific train at Denver's Union Station and settled in for the five-hour trip up the canyon to Fairplay to confront his cousin and tell him the news that he, John, was authorized to accompany Jay down to Denver to await a deputy from Kentucky. Then they would all travel back to Knott County, Kentucky, where Jay would face the music. The October 23, 1898, *Denver Evening Post* described John's demeanor this way:

> "He shall not escape me," said John Draughan, and anybody who saw how stiffly worked his lips, how tense and set his features and how deeply burned the hate beneath his drooping eyelids, knew that he told the truth and that Jay Draughan would not escape.

> "He has killed my father; either the law will punish him or he will die by my hand," said he.

When John arrived at the hospital he was met by Hattie, who, in a dramatic move to dissuade her brother-in-law from transporting her wounded husband, "received him warmly, throwing her arms around his neck and kissing him," according to the *Rocky Mountain News*, September 12, 1897.

However, Jay would have none of it, peeling her arms off his neck and taking a step back from her. She begged him to return home without them, allowing them to "escape" by simply remaining in the quiet Colorado mountain town, but it was all to no avail.

The meeting of the two men occurred that night after Jay's doctor gave his approval. John must have taken great delight in announcing to Jay: "Well, I've got you now!" [*Rocky Mountain News*, September 14, 1897].

Lying prone on a stretcher, Jay was carried to the baggage car of the southbound DSP&P train the next day like a living suitcase. His family at his side, cousin/brother-in-law overseeing all, they arrived at Denver's Union Depot hours later. John loaded his cousin/brother-in-law onto an express wagon, and the family made their way to the city's Occidental Hotel. Jay must have felt like a bag of bones after all the jostling on his trip. John paid for everyone's room expenses – after all, his wife was Hattie's sister.

Shortly after settling in, Jay gave a brief interview to the *Rocky Mountain News*. "John is sore because I killed his father," he admitted contritely, "and I don't blame him." He denied their dispute was over money matters and claimed he could beat the murder charge in Kentucky.

On September 18, 1898, the "big guns" arrived in Denver in the form of the Johnson County sheriff, requisition papers in hand that authorized him to take the wounded suspect back to Kentucky. Sheriff Hays asked that his charge be placed in jail, but the attending doctors denied this request.

Jay's health improved until about a week before the long trip back east was scheduled when he suffered an unexplained relapse. John investigated and claimed that Hattie was giving her husband too much morphine in hopes of delaying their trip as long as possible. He then asked the police surgeon to make a determination on his cousin's ability to travel, which meant yet another delay. Luck was still on Jay's side.

Governor Adams now became involved, ordering the Surgeon General of the Colorado National Guard and another doctor to examine the prisoner. After being medically cleared on October 5, 1897, the Draughn party departed for the long journey back home, with Jay cursing the officers and threatening to take their lives at the first opportunity. On October 21, 1897, in Paintsville, Kentucky, Jay tried to escape. He was shot by the deputies, by John, and by John's younger brother Kell. More than twenty-five bullets were expended, and Jay was again seriously wounded. This was after a judge set aside his bond on the Cunningham case, releasing him from jail there.

On February 3, 1898, Jay stood trial for the murder of Benjamin Cunningham in Paintsville, Kentucky, and was convicted in four hours. One Kentucky newspaper wrote he was sentenced to twenty years in prison while another paper claimed he was sentenced to

PRISONER WHO COULDN'T RESIST.
Hiram Baker captured by his Kentucky cousin on a charge of murder.

An artist's sketch shows John Draughn on the left carrying his cousin Jay on a stretcher with the aid of an unidentified man. Jay's wife stands by with a baby in her arms. *Rocky Mountain News, September 14, 1897*

only ten years for manslaughter. On December 4, 1900, Rory Jay Draughn was pardoned by Governor John Crepps Wickliffe Beckham.

Jay went on to become the Town Marshal of Hazard, Kentucky, where he met his end on December 17, 1912, at 7:30 p.m. in the line of duty. As he tried to arrest a drunken acquaintance, J.O. Combs, who was at the time a candidate for county sheriff, Combs fired four times at close range. The last shot was to the stomach, ironically where Jay had inflicted his mortal wound upon his uncle years earlier. Combs received a life sentence for killing Rory Jay Draughn.

THE MURDER SITE TODAY

The drive up Geneva Gulch is delightful by passenger vehicle. Take the Guanella Pass Road, recently paved in portions from Georgetown to Grant. From the Park County side, it is named County Road (CR 62). Drive north at CR62 from Grant on the well-marked gravel road. At any point between four and seven miles, pull over in a safe place and think about the family feud from long ago.

Hall Valley

"If you want anything to do with us, you had better bring your shooting irons," a Hall Valley "bad man" threatened in August 1873. Little did he know that he and his partner would wind up with "throat trouble" a mere twenty-four hours later in a Hall Valley mining camp, located on today's Park County Road 62.

In the early 1860s, before the valley acquired the Hall name, an adventurer named Scott Shaw prospected the 12,200-foot mountain peaks at the valley's head and discovered the large profitable Whale Mine. Shaw was said to be the son of a French settler and a Spanish woman. He lost a leg in the Civil War and later worked as a U.S. Army scout until he began mining.

Around 1872, a highly decorated Civil War brigadier general, Jairus W. Hall, arrived in the same area after working as a banker and miner in Georgetown for several years after the war. A dashing man with high integrity, he had been partners of sorts with Colonel George Armstrong Custer in 1871 in Clear Creek County. "The Colonel," as Hall was commonly known, purchased the Whale Mine in 1872 for $20,000. British investors financed the extensive smelting works, tramway, and large buildings under construction in anticipation of a massive mining operation. Thus the Hall Valley Silver Lead & Smelting Company was created, and the name Hall Valley referred to the area that the Colonel developed.

During this productive time, and despite Hall's best efforts, the camp soon earned a reputation for lawlessness. It was thirty-five miles from the county's nearest lawman in Fairplay. The *Rocky Mountain News* dubbed the new settlement of Hall Valley "the grand resort of a great majority of unhung rascals."

As with most Colorado boom camps, once the ore played out, the miners abandoned the site in search of mineral wealth elsewhere, and mining towns became ghost towns. Although no buildings remain in the valley today, the area remains rich in Wild West lore. Jairus W. Hall died in 1903 in London, England, where he is buried.

This Hall Valley store may have been the building where Boice and Hall were locked up the night they were lynched. *Courtesy Park County Local History Archives #3229.*

Chapter Eight

DOUBLE TROUBLE
1873

Henry Hall fretted. His little child was sick, and his wife implored him to go get milk from the sawmill at the year-old mining camp called Hall Valley. Of course he wanted to help his child . . . but there was also the ever-constant lure of his saloon just a mile-and-a-half west of the mill.

Hall proceeded to the mill on the morning of August 12, 1873, accompanied by his friend Michael "Big Mike" Boice, who worked on the new tramway that stretched four miles from the Whale Mine down to the smelter. Along the way, they stopped at Brownell's store, purchased whiskey, and started drinking. Hall never made it to the sawmill or back home, and the rest, as they say, is history.

Henry Hall (no relation to Colonel Jairus Hall) hailed from Tennessee and first landed in Omaha, Nebraska, on his trip west, eventually marrying into a well-known family there. Hall and his wife later traveled to Denver, where he engaged in a variety of unknown business ventures; they then drifted up to Fairplay. The couple left Fairplay for Hall Valley after hearing about the Whale silver strike.

Upon arrival, Hall built a saloon and gambling establishment, cornering the liquor market in no time. His good friend Frank Bennett helped him acquire the libations and necessary permits.

The men working to construct Colonel Hall's new mining company grew a little too fond of Henry Hall's wares; to the point it affected their labors and contributed to a lot of brawling. In exasperation, Colonel Hall ordered his employees to stop patronizing the place and fired "the most incorrigible hands," according to the *Rocky Mountain News* of August 16, 1873.

Since the Colonel owned the land the saloon sat on, he ordered Henry Hall to vacate. Henry agreed, in hopes of selling his inventory to the Colonel. If that didn't work, he was going to "bottle the liquors, quit the traffic and go to mining."

Opinions on Henry Hall's character varied. Bennett described his friend as "a quiet, peaceful citizen" who had never been in any trouble whatsoever, let alone killed anyone. However, most newspaper reports claimed that Hall and Boice had killed men before and that on August 12, 1873, they threatened to shoot several civilians, even bragging they would kill Colonel Hall himself.

After the Colonel shut down the saloon, Henry Hall and Boice began shooting up the town, narrowly missing nearby homes. An armed posse of eight men quickly formed to put an end to their nonsense. Sneaking up on Boice and Hall, they ordered the two to "Drop it!" Surprised, the miscreants pulled out their revolvers but saw they were outmatched and threw them down.

A final attempt was made to dissuade the shooters from doing more harm.

"Will you leave the gulch quietly if we let you go?" one of the mine managers asked the two.

The terse reply was, "We will never quit until we are even with you."

With this, some of the Hall Valley Mining Company's officials decided to take the ruffians to the nearest jail, located in Fairplay. Several citizens hitched up a four-mule team, but a quick glance at the late afternoon sun told them they could not complete the trip until well after nightfall. Convinced that Hall and Boice would try to escape under the cover of darkness, the mine officials decided to lock them in an empty storeroom and hold them until morning's first light. Supper was brought to them, and they were left to retire.

Sometime in the dead of night, vigilantes broke into the storeroom, rousted Hall and Boice from their sleep, and took them out into the warm summer air. Both were strung up from nearby trees about a mile south of the sawmill, half a mile down the gulch. The crowd then bought all the whiskey in Hall's saloon and destroyed it by pouring it out or shooting the bottles.

Dawn saw most of the "roughs" of the camp making a quick exodus toward Denver, leaving Hall Valley free of its bad element.

Mining company officials asked Fairplay authorities to appoint a deputy sheriff and a justice of the peace to the district, in an effort to reduce the number of disturbances in the camp.

Bennett was distraught at his friend's death and wrote two letters to the *Rocky Mountain News*. One lamented "a dead child," referring to Hall's child who didn't make it. Bennett's second letter contains the only eyewitness account of the hangings and the burials:

> I then, with three other parties, went to the place where the tragedy was enacted, three-fourths of a mile below the mill and found the two bodies suspended to pines. I cut the bodies down and saw Hall's body buried near the mouth of the gulch. Other parties buried the body of Boice.

The Hall Valley Mining District went on to yield large quantities of silver, lead, and copper, despite initial smelter problems. Like most mines in Park County, the area eventually played out, and the miners moved on.

Colonel Jairus W. Hall was actually a Brigadier General and Civil War veteran, but he preferred to be called Colonel Hall. *Courtesy George Wilkinson and the 4thMichigan.com*

THE HALL VALLEY TOWN SITE TODAY

Hall Valley remains a beautiful valley, easily accessible by car up to the Hall Valley Campground. Head west on Highway 285 from Bailey and turn right onto CR 60 at the base of Kenosha Pass. Drive approximately five miles to the Hall Valley Campground, which is the old town site. Part of the road is privately owned but open to public use. Watch for the signs that clarify restrictions imposed by the land owners.

THE LYNCHING AND BURIAL SITES TODAY

The exact location of the double lynching is unknown. The only location noted in Bennett's letter is "below the mill"—and that Hall was buried at the "mouth of the gulch." This would presumably be soon after the turn onto CR 60, although the road was rerouted in the 1980s. Park at a pull-out wide enough to accommodate a vehicle and imagine where a grave might have been hastily dug.

Chapter Nine

THE CONCORD CHIEF MINE DISPUTE
1886

The *Montezuma Millrun* newspaper account (from neighboring Summit County) of the murder of Hall Valley miner Mike Feeney on August 28, 1886, is brief. The coroner's inquest reports and the eyewitness testimony, however, provided enough information to give a full account of this silver mine feud that ended in a deadly shooting.

The year before his death, Michael "Mike" Feeney contributed $300 worth of labor and improvements to one of his mines named the Concord Chief in 1885. The mine was located in Gibson Gulch, the valley just south of Hall Valley. Frustrated that his partners, Thomas Lambie, John Gallagher, and William Gorman, had not done likewise, he posted a notice of forfeiture in the *Fairplay Flume* on November 5, 1885. The notice stated that unless the partners put some of their own money into the Concord Chief within ninety days, Feeney would take possession of the entire lode. He also posted forfeiture notices on two additional mines: the Metz Lode and the Unknown Lode.

Now, we don't know if this was a "mine grab" scheme on Feeney's part to own the entire operation, or if he was exasperated by the partners' lack of initiative and cooperation. Four years earlier, Feeney had been charged with shenanigans at another mine site. The indictment, dated May 30, 1881, in Park County District Court, alleged: "Michael Feeney did willfully and maliciously remove, pull down and destroy the location stake, side posts and corner posts designating the name of the location and boundaries of the Eureka Lode in the vicinity of Hall's Gulch."

The case was dismissed three months later, but only because "no prosecutor is endorsed thereon by the foreman of the Grand Jury with the consent of the prosecutor." Sounds like Feeney got off on a technicality.

In addition, in October 1883, he had sued Mary B. Cole and won a judgment against her in a jury trial, awarding him $5.95 in damages and "possession of the ground." This was probably a mining disagreement as well.

The fact that little information exists today about the Concord Chief Mine might indicate it was not a big producer, but it is known that the division of ownership was unequal among the four owners.

During his statement at the coroner's inquest panel on August 26, 1886, Gallagher described his conflict with Feeney that began two years before he shot Feeney. "One day as we were sitting in the cabin, Feeney said to me, 'You little son-of-a bitch, I will kill you if you ever work another day in that tunnel.'"

Feeney gave no motive for the threat, but Gallagher was intimidated enough that he went back to town (Hall Valley) the next day and remained there, for two years, until the summer of 1896. In August, he returned to the mine tunnel only to find his enemy also working there.

"Hello, Mike," said Gallagher. "Could I look at the face of the tunnel?"

"Yes," was the reply.

While Gallagher was peering inside, Feeney retrieved his gun and pointed it at his enemy.

"You little son-of-a-bitch, get out of here!" Feeney said, raising his voice.

Gallagher told the rest of the story to the coroner's panel:

He called me other hard names. He pointed the gun at me and run me out of the tunnel, following me clean out to the dump [the tailings]. Mike said, "If you ever come back here, I will kill you." He threw his gun down on the ground and said, "I will whip you anyhow." I went away from him and did not go back to the tunnel again until yesterday (August 25,1886) when I came and met co-owner Thomas Lambie on the dump and went in the tunnel with him.

Once in the mine, Gallagher said to Feeney, "How do you do, Mike. Can I come to work?"

"No, you son-of-a- bitch," hollered Feeney, pulling out his gun.

"Don't shoot, Mike!" yelled Bill Gorman, but it was too late. Feeney pulled the trigger. The three bolted and ducked for cover behind the ore car inside the tunnel as Feeney fired again. Gallagher had had enough, and he returned fire. In his words:

> Then I started shooting. There was a light near Feeney when I fired. He grabbed the candlestick and started towards me and I ran towards the dump. My shoulder struck against a timber and I fell down. I turned as soon as I could and saw Feeney with the light and began shooting again. I went out of the tunnel a ways further and heard some more shots and I kept on shooting until my gun was emptied. I ran out of the tunnel and met Lambie on the dump. I did not stop until I got to Hall Valley. I did not know whether I had hit Feeney or not until I came up today. My other partners wanted me to go to work in the tunnel. I carried a gun because I was afraid of Feeney. I did not shoot until Feeney had fired two shots.

After the dust settled, Lambie and Gorman, cautiously crept back up to where Feeney lay, crumpled by numerous bullets. Gorman testified: "There seemed to be some life in him when we found him. We placed him in the car and brought him outside. He was dead when we got out to the dump."

It is not known whether the body was brought down the mountain—perhaps on a burro—or buried near the mine.

Gallagher did not find out until later that four of the six bullets fired at Feeney had hit their deadly mark. Dr. Charles H. Scott, the county coroner, logged a detailed report of the fatal wounds on August 26, 1886.

Because Gallagher did not fire first, and because Feeney had threatened him over the course of two years, the jurors at the coroner inquest decided, "that the said shooting and killing was done in self-defense and wholly justifiable and the said John Gallagher is exonerated from all blame."

Case closed.

THE MURDER SITE TODAY

The exact location of the Concord Chief Mine within Gibson Gulch is unknown. Hiking Gibson Gulch in search of the mine is not a casual hike! It is a highly strenuous hike for even the most seasoned mountaineers. Hikers must be acclimated to Colorado's high altitude because the three-mile hike ends at almost 12,000 feet. In addition, the hiker will need a four-wheel-drive vehicle to get to the Gibson Lake trail, located approximately 1.2 miles beyond the Hall Valley Campground on CR 60. Drive through the creek to a turnout on the left marked Gibson Lake. Park in the turnout, which is the trailhead. Follow the trail up the gulch and imagine for yourself the location of the Concord Chief.

Chapter Ten

HALL VALLEY POISON
1883

This exciting tale has all the makings of a classic western, complete with a man shot in the back, a comical jail break, and a probable shoot-out in Wyoming.

Amos Brazille had been in Colorado only two days when he was murdered by Jacob Byard (or Bayard). Brazille was a young fellow who came out west from his family home in Rockport, Missouri, on October 13, 1883. He stood over six feet tall, a "stately presence" (according to the *Fairplay Flume*, October 18, 1883), but his congenial personality helped temper his intimidating size. He had been pretty "boozy" most of his short time in the Hall Valley mining camp and had laughed off his two recent scrapes with other residents.

On the night of October 15, he was in George Campbell's saloon with Jacob Byard, the new foreman of the Ypsilanti Mine, which was located at the head of the valley. Byard, aka "Big Jake," age twenty-nine, had lived in Colorado for five years and had been a miner at the Ypsilanti. When word of his promotion got out, there was grumbling from his co-workers, so Byard bought a .44 Colt revolver in case of trouble.

Byard had promised Brazille a mining job. That night, they played cards until 11 p.m. and seemed to get along fine, in spite of the banter of who could "whip" who.

"Why, you couldn't whip me even if you had a gun," grinned Brazille, then jokingly accused Byard of stealing poker chips. Another saloon patron saw the two shake hands, and it appeared all differences were settled. Bartender Stephen H. Russell overheard Brazille ask Byard if he could bunk with him that night.

The site of the Ypsilanti Mine is located near the top of Hall Valley. Murderer Jacob Byard worked at the Ypsilanti. *Courtesy Park County Local History Archives*

"The ground is good enough for the likes of you," was Byard's retort, and suddenly the tone of friendship soured.

"But I was expecting to stay with you," Brazille complained.

Shoving his chair out from under him, Byard drew up his large frame, stepped outside in the cool night air, and walked up the hill a ways. Brazille followed briefly, but then returned to the comforts of the saloon and whiskey. "Go and get that poor boy. I believe he is drunk," he joked with the bartender.

Byard came back to the saloon, with his new revolver in his coat. When Byard entered the saloon, Brazille called out, "Come and have a drink with me."

"Not right now," Byard replied.

Byard again went outside and in a few minutes, turned around, cracked the door open halfway, and stood on the top step of the saloon, and shouted, "God damn you, take that!" From five feet away, he plugged Brazille in the side, with the victim's back to him—the lowest form of killing in the unwritten code of the West.

"For God's sake, boys, he has killed me!" Brazille cried out.

The bartender and saloon owner George Campbell immediately snatched the gun away from Byard.

"Turn that gun loose!" demanded the murderer.

"I won't do it—you have killed a man," hollered Campbell. With that, Byard turned and walked out of the saloon minus his weapon.

"Hold me, I am falling," sputtered the mortally wounded man. Campbell helped Brazille onto the floor. Blood soon soaked the wood planks. "Please write to my father and tell him that the long son-of-a-bitch has killed me."

Russell ran out to get the doctor, but by the time the two returned, Brazille was dead. He had lingered only thirty minutes.

Where did the shooter go that night? Initially, he hid out in the nearby ore smelter, then walked back into town the next morning. When told the man he shot was dead, Byard replied, "I better take a walk." And walk he did—toward the nearby town of Webster, leaving his footprints in the snow.

Two mounted and armed citizens, O. C. Mugrage and James Rawls, were hot on his tail. They spotted Byard near Webster and apprehended him as he darted into the bushes. Byard went quietly with his captors to Webster, where Mugrage and Rawls swore out a complaint in front of Justice of the Peace J. J. Smith, whose own troubles with the law are the subject of Chapter 11. Smith deputized Mugrage and Rawls, and the three men hauled Byard by wagon down the long road to Fairplay and an awaiting jail cell.

Byard just missed the October 1883 term of court, so he would now have to wait seven months until Judge William Harrison rode back into Fairplay for the May 1884 session. The county jail was nine-years old and by no means escape-proof. One out-of-towner joked that the inmates should wear "pig-yokes" to keep them from slipping through all the holes.

The county jailer should have known to keep an eye on the cell bars, because a notorious cattle rustler Ernest Christison had filed away on one of the bars during his confinement in 1883. After he found Christison's small saw, Byard picked up where the former inmate had left off. He sawed on the bars at night, literally in concert with an inmate who was allowed to play his fiddle after dinner. Byard cut a ten-by-sixteen-inch hole that allowed him and all the

State of Colorado
Park County

s

At an inquisition holden
at Hall Valley in Park county
on the 16th day of October 1883.
before James J Smith J. P.
of said county, upon the
dead body of E Brazielle, lying
there dead, by the jurors whose
names are hereto subscribed;
the said jurors do say that
the said E Brazielle came
to his death from a shot
from a 45 calibre colts revolver
from the hand of Jacob Byard
and said shot was fired
feloniously and with murder
=ous intent —
In testimony whereof The said
jurors have hereunto set their
hands the day and year aforesaid.

J A Tracy   Forman
H. D. Finn
J S Wyett
John Herrmann
Eben S Mely
P J Fleming

other inmates (save one who decided to stay put) to spill out into freedom at 1:00 a.m. on March 19, 1884.

Byard and fellow prisoner Charles Buck disappeared into the darkness, but Frank Record, the fiddler jailed with Byard, dutifully presented himself at the sheriff's home to inform the lawman of the latest events at the jail. Men on horseback tracked the jailbirds but had no luck. The *Rocky Mountain News* dubbed the story "Big Jake's Break" on March 20, 1884.

Sheriff William Burns went to Denver and Colorado Springs for assistance, offering a $100 reward, later increasing it to $500. *The Flume* of March 27, 1884, offered the following description of the outlaw:

> He is six feet and six inches in height; if so, we will say he does not look it; still, he is a giant in stature and would find it impossible to disguise his height. He looks to be about thirty-five years of age and has one forefinger, we believe, missing and one middle finger crooked. The marks are hard to disguise.

One month later, Deputy Sheriff George Nyce traced Byard to Buffalo, Wyoming, after tailing him for two weeks. Byard was holed up with relatives in a small cabin near Buffalo and heavily armed. Byard's father had vacated his cabin in Park County around the time of Brazille's murder. Did he help his son escape and go on the run with him up to Wyoming?

Although the April 22, 1884, *Rocky Mountain News* caption proclaimed "Murderer Recaptured," the reporter leaves the reader hanging by not saying whether "Big Jake" Byard was indeed corralled or if he was killed in the likely shootout with Nyce. Byard's name never appears in the *Flume* again, leaving us to assume he was not brought to justice in a Colorado courtroom. Or perhaps he was, but the story was not deemed newsworthy for some reason. The 1886 and 1887 issues of the Flume are missing. Bayard could have stood trial during that time. The outlaw's ultimate destiny remains unknown to this day.

A rare Coroner's report. It lists victim Amos Brazille's cause of death as " a shot from a 45 caliber colt s revolver from the hand of Jacob Byard." *Courtesy Park County Local History Archives*

Not much remains of the Hall Valley Smelter, used to treat the silver ores from the rich mines at the top of the gulch. Big Jake hid out here after he shot and killed Amos Brazille. *Courtesy Christie Wright*

THE MURDER SITE TODAY

The town of Hall Valley was located approximately at the site of the present-day Hall Valley Campground. Drive up Hall Valley Road (CR 60) five miles and follow the signs to the campground, which bears left at an intersection. Although no structures or foundations remain, this was the site of a lively mining town in its time.

THE PARK COUNTY JAIL TODAY

The jail that Byard escaped from stands today just west of the old Fairplay courthouse. The jail is sometimes open to the public during the annual Fairplay Burro Days, held the last weekend in July. It is worth a trip to Fairplay to see the cells and walls, and the July burro race is most enjoyable to watch.

The Smith and Grow ranches were located in this area near the mouth of Hall Valley. *Courtesy Christie Wright*

Chapter Eleven

PARK COUNTY'S HATFIELDS and McCOYS—1885

In the mid-1870s, settlers John W. Grow and James J. "J. J." Smith started a way station on the Bradford and Blue River Toll Road, at the site of the present-day Highway 285 in Webster. Over the years, the business devolved into only a boardinghouse, called the Webster House. It was considered one of the finer hotels in the county. On the night of February 28, 1883, when it caught fire and was destroyed, the loss was keenly felt by the surrounding communities.

Grow and Smith rebuilt after the fire, but the partnership "went south," and squabbles turned into heated arguments that ultimately led to the dissolution of the business. Bitter feelings spilled over into the courtroom, when the two filed several civil lawsuits against each other.

One thing that did not change was the locations of the ex-partners' ranches. J. J. Smith had purchased his homestead in 1882 at the mouth of Hall Valley. Grow's spread was nestled adjacent and to the east.

On the morning of July 2, 1885, things came to a tragic head. Hattie Grow, John's eight-year-old daughter, was driving some of her father's cattle up the public Hall Valley Road by Smith's property when Smith's mother, Catherine, came out of the cabin and tried turning the cattle back. The animals had recently made a mess of J.J.'s new oat field—which was not fenced because painful rheumatism had kept him from completing the task. Mrs. Smith did not want the cattle tramping the field yet again.

J. J. joined his mother in trying to turn the herd across a bridge toward nearby Kenosha Gulch, whereupon John Grow and his wife, Sallie, entered the fray, and forced the cattle back in their original

James J. Smith was sentenced to ten years in prison for killing his neighbor, William. R. Grow. After he was pardoned, Smith went on to become a justice of the peace and a mine owner. *Courtesy Colorado State Archives*

direction. A "herding contest" was now on between the Grows and the Smiths, with each family trying to turn the cattle in opposite directions. They upped their efforts by throwing rocks at the beasts and at each other. J. J. called Sallie Grow a "son-of-a-bitch" and looked as if he were going to throw a rock at her face.

It seemed unlikely that two highly regarded Hall Valley couples would be engaged in a scene such as this. However, as a July 9, 1885, *Fairplay Flume* article explained, "The situation would appear ridiculous but for the deep significance it had to these people, who hated each other with an undying hate."

The rock throwing led to J. J. pulling a gun and shooting John in the face at close range.

Sallie screamed, "Stop!" and ran to J. J., threw one arm around his neck, and tackled him to the ground. John Grow slumped onto their thrashing bodies. J. J. later testified to the coroner that he was still holding the gun. Then, with Mrs. Grow's grip holding his wrist, J.

J. put the gun to her husband's breast and fired again. The coroner's report later determined, "Grow was no better than a dead man after the first shot."

Witnesses who ran to the scene included railroad agent J. D. Lee, N. C. Estabrook, and two boarders at the Smith house. Sobbing, Mrs. Grow helped the two men and others carry her husband's lifeless form back to their house, where they "laid him on the bed. Lee pulled off his boots and placed a guard over the body. There was no revolver or other weapon upon his person."

Miners, Hall Valley citizens, and residents from up and down the canyon came to the scene as soon as they heard the news. One man rode sixty-three miles in the cold and rain to get there. Grow was a prominent businessman, and final respects were certainly in order.

J. J. Smith's version of the shooting, as provided to a *Flume* newspaper correspondent on July 9, 1885, was that he shot Grow in the breast because he feared Mrs. Grow would stab him, then, "Soon after, he mounted a horse and started for Fairplay, first telegraphing the authorities here that he was coming to give himself up."

Smith's story was full of holes because Grow was known not to carry a weapon, especially a knife, and no weapon was found on or near the body after his death. J. J. told the reporter that he returned home after the shooting. His mother later testified that he tried to eat breakfast but was unable to because his hands were too bloody.

A coroner's jury was convened the day of the shooting and determined Smith fired his weapon "feloniously." He was detained and a preliminary examination resulted in him being held at the county jail in Fairplay without bail. No doubt this businessman-turned-miner was counting on making bond instead of being jailed like a common criminal.

Bond was later set and J. J. posted the required portion of the $10,000 bail approximately one week later, and his trial was held in October 1886. Because the 1886 and 1887 issues of the *Fairplay Flume* are unavailable, that newspaper's take on the story is unknown. Summit County's *Montezuma Millrun* newspaper, dated October 23, 1886, reported that James J. Smith was found guilty and sentenced to ten years in prison. An old volume at the Colorado

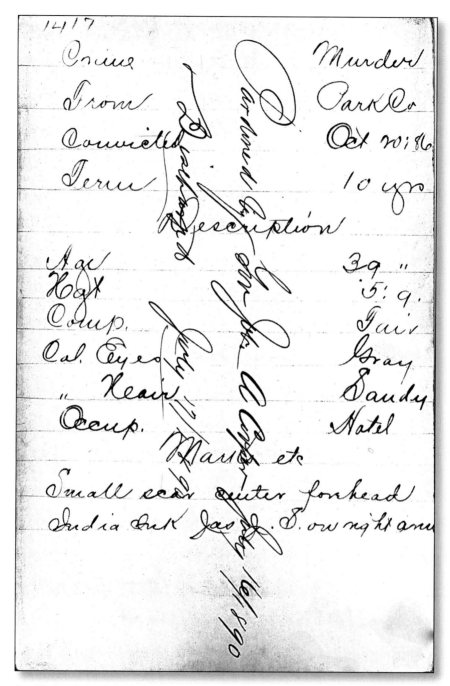

Smith's Bio Sheet from DOC *Courtesy Colorado State Archives*

Department of Corrections titled, *Record of Convicts When Received in the United States Penitentiary for Colorado*, tells the story. There, Smith is listed as an inmate, sentenced to ten years' confinement for murder, but later pardoned on July 16, 1890.

Smith returned to the Webster area and became postmaster, justice of the peace, and a mine owner. (Ironically, he owned the Ypsilanti Mine, where seven years earlier, Jacob Byard was superintendent. See Chapter 10.) In addition, he deterred a murder in Grant in 1902 at his friend Charles Combs's saloon. (See Chapter 3).

James J. Smith died suddenly on April 22, 1912, at age sixty-eight while visiting a friend in Webster. His obituary says he was one of the most "highly respected residents of the Webster and Hall Valley District."

We are left to wonder if John Grow's family would agree.

THE MURDER SITE TODAY

From newspaper descriptions, Smith shot Grow near Hall Valley Road and the railroad tracks, although the tracks no longer exist. The easiest way to get to the site is to turn up Hall Valley Road (CR 60) from Highway 285 at the east base of Kenosha Pass. There is a pull-out on the right, just a few yards after the turn onto CR 60. All the surrounding area is private property and trespassing is not allowed.

This sawmill near Beaver Gulch is typical and is probably very similar to the sawmill where Charles Brymer may have worked. Logging was an important Park County industry at the turn of the century. *Courtesy Park County Local History Archives. Source: Helen Purinton Jones.*

Chapter Twelve

BAD BLOOD in BEAVER GULCH
1894

Nineteen-year-old Charles Brymer was furious, and for good reason. After working hard for tie camp boss John Smedley near the mouth of Hall Valley, Brymer had yet to be paid one red cent. Coming to Colorado from Olympia, Washington, "Charley" had landed himself a job in 1894 in one of the Hall Valley area camps where ties were made for the expanding railroad lines—a vital Park County industry from the 1800s to mid-1900s.

Smedley's failure to pay Brymer would be his undoing. Other workers were in the same plight with their bosses, but Brymer vowed that Smedley was not going to get away with it. Brymer had asked for his pay about six weeks earlier, only to be met with the swing of an axe at his head.

"If you ask again, I'll kill you!" Smedley allegedly shouted at the time.

Obviously a simple request was not going to work, so the disgruntled but determined Brymer walked sixty miles from Webster to Denver to purchase a Colt .41 caliber revolver. No one was going to take advantage of Charley Brymer!

When he returned to Platte Canyon on November 20, 1894, Brymer's first stop was in nearby Geneva Gulch to accost a former boss named William Tate, who owed Brymer eighteen dollars. The *Rocky Mountain News* of November 21, 1894, reported their spying.

> On meeting Tate about two miles above here, the latter told Brymer that he was then shipping a carload of wood to Denver with the express intention of paying the money from

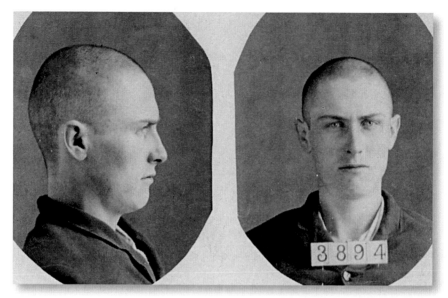

Nineteen year-old Charles Brymer's mug shot. Brymer was sentenced to prison for killing his supervisor, John Smedley. *Courtesy Colorado State Archives*

the returns. He asked Brymer to go back to his house and stay there until the money came. Brymer then changed his mind about killing Tate.

This promise of money must have satisfied the gun-toting lumberman, because Tate lived to tell the coroner his version of Brymer's activities.

Brymer struck out on foot for Beaver Gulch, the next gulch over, where Beaver Creek runs. The area is aptly named for numerous beaver ponds can be seen all up and down the little valley. On his way, he met up with several acquaintances, one being W. A. Carbonn.

"Do you know where Smedley is?" Brymer inquired.

"No, I saw him and his teamster go up the road toward Beaver Gulch," was the reply. Carbonn saw the gun sticking out from Brymer's hip pocket.

Three hours later, around 4 p.m., Brymer came upon two friends, Chris Robinson and William L. Shaffer, who were cutting timber near the mouth of Beaver Gulch. Brymer asked Shaffer if he knew where Smedley was.

"No," said Shaffer, pausing, "I did not see him yesterday at all."

"I want to see him and if I do, the son-of-a-bitch will never come out of that gulch a live man!" spat Brymer. The conversation ended casually with Brymer announcing, "I believe I will go up and work for Jack Filch cutting wood."

Robinson later testified that soon thereafter, he heard three shots and saw gun smoke rise from about one-and-one-half miles away up the valley. Twenty minutes later, Smedley's teamster, J. R. Maynor, came down on horseback, and told Robinson and Shaffer that Smedley had been killed.

Maynor, who had worked only two weeks for the deceased, witnessed the entire affair. He told the coroner's inquest panel that about 3 p.m. he and Smedley were coming down the gulch with Smedley riding the brake on the big wagon with himself (Maynor) riding on top of the load, driving the team. Maynor went on to testify, "I see a man come up the road. He walked up to the wagon, pulled his gun and shot Mr. Smedley, whose back was toward him." Maynor also testified that Smedley dropped to the ground and staggered toward his murderer, pleading, "Oh my God, Charley don't shoot me anymore!" Brymer fired two more shots. Smedley fell to the ground and never uttered another word.

After the shooting, Maynor recounted: "The man [Brymer] came over to me and said: 'I worked for that man,' waving his gun towards Smedley, and words to the effect that the dead man needed to pay for what he had done." Maynor testified that Brymer then turned and walked up the road.

Brymer walked to a house belonging to W. A. George near the mouth of the creek arriving around 6 p.m. George was not home, but his son Frank and a friend, Mr. Bolton, were. Brymer asked for shelter for the night. After hearing his confession that he had shot and killed Smedley, the two insisted that he throw down his arms. Brymer refused.

At 7 p.m., George arrived home to find a criminal in his midst. He, too, heard the story of the shooting and spoke at length with Brymer. He encouraged the young man to turn himself in to the law in Fairplay. Finally, at 5 a.m., an exhausted Charley Brymer threw down his Colt and knife and agreed to go with Bolton to the county seat to avoid what surely would have been a lynching.

One year later, in November 1895, a verdict of second-degree murder put the shooter behind bars in Canon City, Colorado, for eight years. He served approximately five years and was discharged on January 30, 1901.

John Smedley left behind a wife and five young children to fend for themselves. They eventually required the county to step in and support them as paupers for a time.

THE MURDER SITE TODAY

Today, Beaver Gulch is used primarily as a four-wheel drive road and a popular ATV road. Do not attempt to drive this road in a passenger car. A few miles into the gulch, the road becomes very steep and rutty. On maps, the road is named CR 202, but there is no posted signage.

Drive three miles west Hall Valley Road (CR60) and take the first left at a brown wooden sign that says "Beaver Creek—Road Ends 4½." The road leads through a steep, rocky area—probably the same area where Brymer murdered his boss. Visualize a loaded timber wagon pulled by a horse team traversing this steep grade.

Notice the thick forest on either side, possibly this was the site of old lumbering operations. The road opens up into a flat area, then climbs higher, past many beaver ponds on the left, to a dead-end. Watch for moose in these lush areas. There is a large loop turn-around at the dead-end.

The Northern Ranches

With the mining booms came a need for meat and grains to feed the swelling populations in the camps. Ranchers, many of them with new homestead parcels of 160 acres, were happy to provide the provisions. The northern part of the South Park was ideal for both cattle and hay, and the choice land was soon claimed along with the water rights. Ranching was difficult when drought set in or when the winter season had heavy snows.

The 1870s were the county's heyday of ranching. Open range (or free grazing) was the norm until the railroads began to cross the South Park—the Midland from the east and the Denver, South Park & Pacific from the north. Then fencing was required to keep the livestock safe.

The Michigan Creek area, which begins north of Como on the north flank of Mount Guyot and continues along the broad plain east of Highway 285, proved to be profitable and popular for ranching. There, large spreads such as the Wahl-Coleman Ranch, the Baker Ranch, the Wadley sheep ranch at Red Hill, and others contributed to feeding the local population.

The Jefferson depot photographed in the late 1930s. Uplide Vallie worked at the depot as the ticket agent in the early 1900s. *Courtesy Park County Local History Archives # 1719. Source: South Park Historical Foundation.*

Chapter Thirteen

WAS A MURDERESS ACQUITTED?
1902

Ella J. Koons was raised a proper young lady in a proper, church-going home in Logansport, Indiana. She sang in the church choir, played the piano, and had perfect grammar school attendance. Her father, John M. Koons, was a prosperous farmer and her mother was a member of the local Ladies' Aid Society. When her parents moved to Springfield, Missouri, in 1888 to be near their oldest daughter, Mary, who had recently married, Ella remained in Indiana.

In her early twenties, Ella chose to use one of the popular matrimonial agencies of the time. Through the agency, she met an older rancher named Uplide Vallie. The couple married in Clinton, Iowa, on April 20, 1887, then moved to Jefferson, Colorado, where "Lide" Vallie established a homestead. He also worked for the local railroad as a ticket agent at the Jefferson train depot, a convenient arrangement that allowed him to walk home at the end of his shift.

Because his station agent duties did not leave much time for ranch work, Vallie hired a ranch manager and extra ranch hands during the fall haying season. One of Vallie's hands was twenty-six-year-old Charles Ulay Baker, who came to Colorado from Michigan. Baker first worked in the South Park hay fields during the fall of 1900 and upon his return the following summer, Vallie hired him. After haying season, the two settled up Baker's wages on September 28, 1901. There was a minor disagreement over the amount—Baker claimed Vallie owed him an extra dollar—but it was resolved when Vallie agreed to the additional pay. Baker was then hired at Charles Pemberton's ranch nearby.

On the evening of October 9, 1901, Uplide Vallie never made it home from the depot. His bludgeoned body was found the next morning 150 feet from his house.

The murder followed the triple homicide of three school board members by Benjamin Ratliff six years earlier in the Bordenville area, eleven miles southeast of Jefferson. (See Chapter 14.) Vallie's demise traumatized the local residents once again, causing fear and speculation until Baker was arrested approximately one week later as a suspect. There was a second and more personal reason for speculation about the homicide. Rumors swirled of a possible "intrigue" between the attractive Mrs. Vallie and the younger Baker.

A coroner's inquest was immediately held to determine the manner of death. Witness George Overholt, who found the body, testified that the victim had suffered six blows to the head. A wooden cane was believed to be the murder weapon after strips of varnished wood were discovered near the victim. This find was important because the cane was made of hickory, a hardwood not found in Colorado. The jury also delved into the conflicts that the victim may have had with other acquaintances to see if other suspects might surface.

When it was Mrs. Vallie's turn to testify, she denied having an affair with Baker but did admit her husband had cautioned her against taking wagon rides into town with Baker. She clarified that her husband made the request about the wagon rides only because Mr. Vallie thought people would "talk." Mrs. Vaille claimed it was nothing more than a "minor disagreement" between her and her husband.

The coroner's inquest concluded, "The said Uplide Vallie came to his death by reason of blows inflicted on his head and body by one Charles Baker on or about the 9th day of October, A.D. 1901 in the County of Park and State of Colorado and that said killing was felonious."

The evidence against Baker was two-fold: First, he was seen in possession of a heavy wooden cane the previous week in a Jefferson saloon. During his testimony, he admitted that he had recently purchased the cane in Denver but had left it in the saloon. Second, blood-stained clothing belonging to Baker was found in the Vallie home on October 17, 1901, when District Attorney Augustus Pease, Charles Pemberton, and Peter Lapham conducted a search

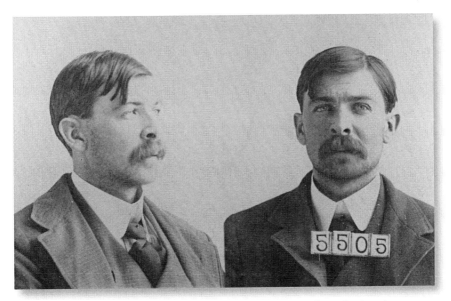

Young Charles Baker's mug shot was taken at the Colorado State Penitentiary on August 17, 1902. Note the stick pin in the knot of his tie. Baker lived to 87 and is buried in Michigan. *Courtesy Colorado State Archives*

of the home for evidence. (Lapham was one of the witnesses who had seen Baker in the saloon with the cane.)

The clothing included a corduroy coat and matching vest that had recently been washed but still had blood stains. The vest had been cut into strips and stuffed into several locations—in the outhouse, in an unused stove, and in some wall cracks. Baker's coat, with a stick pin fastened to the lapel, was found. These suspicious items could have been planted while Mrs. Vallie was in Denver. In addition, Baker claimed his clothing had recently been stolen from Pemberton's ranch.

District Attorney "Gus" Pease issued a warrant for Ella's arrest on October 11, 1901, because the incriminating clothing was found in her house. She was not arrested at home because she and two friends had left by train earlier that day to accompany her husband's body to Denver for burial in Fairmont Cemetery. When Mrs. Vallie stepped off the Union Station platform that evening, two Denver deputies arrested her as a crowd gathered to watch.

The *Fairplay Flume* of October 18, 1901, provided the following description of her detainment:

She did not evince the least surprise when arrested, but
calmly listened to the officers' words, and without so much
as expressing a desire to see her husband's body safely cared
for, prepared to accompany the officers to the jail. She was
driven to the county jail in a closed carriage, but kept silent
during the ride to the jail.

Mrs. Vallie's stoic façade served to heighten suspicions about her
involvement in her husband's murder. She appeared to be detached
and uninterested in either her husband's death or her own predica-
ment. The *Flume* even speculated on her sanity, opining that she
was either "faking her detachment or was mentally deranged." The
Denver newspapers flocked to the theory, sending reporters—
including one female reporter named Kitty Lee—to the jail to interview the inmate. During the interviews, Ella casually draped herself
on a sofa in the matron's lounge, claiming a headache. Shielding
her eyes with her hand, she seemed to alternately enjoy and dislike
the attention and newspaper photographers, one minute worrying if
her hair was in place and the next, refusing to answer any questions.
She asked the *Denver Times* photographer to send her one of his
photos of her, but only if it was a good likeness.

The next day, Sheriff Silas Polluck arrived in Denver to transport
the widow back to the Park County jail. Although he had previously
hinted he would allow Ella to attend her husband's funeral, he now
refused. This caused Mrs. Vallie to exclaim in dismay:

> I'll walk all the way back if we miss the train, if you want me
> to. Anything you say, if you will let me see him once more,
> all alone without anyone near. I do not want to stay for the
> funeral when everyone will be there, but just alone for a few
> minutes, if no more.

But the funeral went on without her. The only flowers were
those that the women's jail matron, Mrs. Walker, placed on the
coffin at Ella's request. Ella had slipped some money to the female
guard to purchase the bouquets just before Polluck whisked her
back to Fairplay.

Mrs. Vallie's preliminary examination was held on October 18,
1901. She was dressed in heavy mourning clothes, and her stoicism

Ella Vallie draped herself across the arm of a couch in the matron's office of the Denver jail for newspaper interviews. She alternately enjoyed and seemed indifferent to the publicity that came with the trial. *Denver Times,* October 12, 1901

had changed to intermittent weeping throughout the proceedings. No evidence was introduced to connect her to the crime, and she was released. Young Baker did not fare as well; he was bound over for trial. Bail was denied. Although he requested a special term of the court for his trial to be conducted, this, too, was denied forcing him to remain in jail for six months until the next District Court session.

Mrs. Vallie's lawyer, Judge Hilton of Denver, made a startling announcement that was published in the *Denver Times* on October, 20, 1901. He claimed that two new suspects living in Jefferson had come to light; that Uplide Vallie had at least one sworn enemy and that the murder weapon was possibly a heavy iron instrument and not a wooden stick. Pinkerton detectives claimed they had unearthed one man in particular whom Vallie was "in mortal fear of," according to Hilton's newspaper interview. Hilton also expounded on the theory that the blood-stained clothing was planted. This was consistent with Baker's assertion that his clothes were stolen

from Pemberton's barn and that Ella would not have left her house
knowing the items were there.

In a second stunning turn of events, Mrs. Vallie was rearrested
on October 23, 1901, after District Attorney Pease claimed to have
new evidence that would convict both Baker and Ella Vallie. The
evidence was never revealed to the public, but Ella remained in jail
until mid-December when she was finally able to post bond.

In May 1902, Baker was more than ready for his day in court,
but his trial was continued for a special session until August. His
attorney was a former Park County prosecutor, M. J. Bartley, who
had an excellent reputation and who had defended Benjamin
Ratcliff several years earlier. The sensational trial began on Tuesday,
August 12, 1902, after jury selection, which took three days. The trial
itself lasted only until August 14, when the verdict came back at
noon, less than twenty-four hours after the jury began deliberations.

"Guilty of second degree murder, Your Honor," was the foreman's pronouncement. The verdict required a prison sentence at
the court's discretion of between ten years and life. Judge Bailey
imposed a term of thirty-five to sixty years. Dressed in his suit with
the stick pin in his lapel, Charles Ulay Baker was taken to Canon
City forthwith.

Two months after her alleged lover was sentenced to prison,
Ella Vallie's trial began on October 24, 1902. Mrs. Vallie did not
shed any tears in the courtroom this time around. Nevertheless, the
verdict was "not guilty." Whatever new convincing evidence Pease
claimed he had was either insufficient or never made public.

Baker was released on parole on May 27, 1918, after serving 16
years in prison; he discharged his sentence on November 17, 1930, at
the age of 54. Returning to his home state of Michigan, he married, and
at some point, moved to Wyoming, where he died in 1971 at age 87.

Ella Koons Vallie married her ranch foreman, George W. Clark,
in February 1907 in Springfield, Missouri, where her sister lived.
Upon returning to Colorado, Ella cleverly converted the Vallie land
deeds to her new married name, providing the couple with considerable ranch land, although Clark owned almost 160 acres in his
own right. In 1912, the Clarks purchased the 640-acre homestead
southeast of Jefferson. Most of the couple's ranch buildings burned
down after cinders from the Denver, South Park & Pacific Railroad

caught the dry winter grass along the tracks on fire. From there, the trail grows murky as to where they lived out their later years.

The murder of Uplide Vallie remains one of Park County's mysteries, replete with numerous possible scenarios. Did Pemberton plant incriminating evidence in the deceased's home to implicate Mrs. Vallie? Was he the murderer? Or did Pemberton pay one of his ranch hands to steal Baker's clothes and plant them in Vallie's house? Could Ella have disguised herself as a man and murdered her husband? It seems doubtful she would have the strength to bludgeon a grown man to death, yet the *Denver Republican* newspaper published this theory October 12, 1901. What happened to the two Jefferson suspects that Judge Hilton was so sure would be arrested? Whom did Vallie fear? Was Charles Baker framed? Did the jury acquit a murderess?

THE MURDER SITE TODAY

The Vallie ranch contained several land parcels but in general was located just north of Michigan Hill, west of Jefferson. Today the land is privately owned, but the area can be viewed by driving west out of central Jefferson on Michigan Creek Road, located just north of the blue depot. After the road bears to the left, turn right onto Jefferson Lake Road, which ends at Jefferson Lake.

The logs visible today at the site where Benjamin Ratcliff shot and killed his victims are not remnants of the Michigan Creek school. Other structures have stood on the same location, including the Centerville Ranger Station from 1908 to 1910. *Courtesy Sean Brubaker, Evoke Images*

Chapter Fourteen

THE RATCLIFF MURDERS
1895

The big keys rattled and grated in the iron locks and the steel latticed door opened slowly. The warden stepped in and read the death warrant. The white-haired old man listened in silence, bowing his head slightly when the warden had finished. . . . He died as he lived—without showing the least sign of fear and met death with that stoical indifference that has marked his behavior since the commission of the crime last May.

So wrote a *Rocky Mountain News* reporter on February 8, 1896, the evening of Benjamin Ratcliff's execution. Benjamin Ratcliff (sometimes spelled Radcliff) was the only Park County man to be legally executed at the Colorado State Penitentiary in the nineteenth century. (Cicero C. Sims was the only man legally executed by the county; the State took over the task in 1889.)

Why the fifty-four-year old rancher shot and killed three school board members in a schoolhouse on the Tarryall Road is still not known with certainty. Extensive genealogy information, available from his descendants in a 2010 book titled *The Legend of Benjamin Ratcliff*, provides excellent background material and some behavioral insights.

Ratcliff grew up on a Missouri farm with seven siblings, raised by parents Elias Ratcliff and Elizabeth Dutcher. At age nineteen, he joined the Union army and was assigned as a wagon master with the Missouri Cavalry. He was badly injured in the Battle of Shiloh when his horse rolled down a hillside. (Later surgeries helped repair the damage to his leg and hip, but he suffered from the war injuries

throughout his life.) He was taken prisoner in August 1864 during
the Confederates' effort to capture St. Louis, Missouri, but he
escaped two days later. He returned to the family farm for a time.
In addition to farming, he was employed as a railroad inspector and
did some "riding for the State of Missouri after outlaws," probably
as a bounty hunter.

Six years after the end of the Civil War, in June 1871, he married
Elizabeth McNair, who lived nearby. The couple struck out for
Colorado that fall, settling in the Tarryall area northwest of Lake
George. The couple homesteaded, raising cattle and hay. Ratcliff
participated in the Republican caucus and joined a ranchers' associ-
ation. In 1892, he was responsible for nominating a man named
Samuel Taylor for county commissioner. Taylor would later
become one of his murder victims.

Ratcliff seemed to have more than his share of conflicts in the
county. These were occasionally mentioned in the local newspaper
and were used against him in his 1895 trial. One episode involved
neighbor Charles Dunbar, who objected to the location of Ratcliff's
ranch buildings—even though Ratcliff built them near the previous
owner's structures. Another conflict arose with neighbor Timothy
Borden, who sued Ratcliff over a road right-of-way; Ratcliff took the
matter to jury trial and was found not guilty. Ratcliff also lost a cow
when someone cut the animal's hamstring, other cows were run off,
his saddle horse was purposely cut under the saddle blanket, and
his guns filled with sand.

These were trifling matters compared to his two biggest chal-
lenges during this time: his children's education and a nasty rumor
about his oldest teenage daughter.

Three years after arriving in Park County, Benjamin and
Elizabeth started their family. Three children were born: a son
in 1874, and daughters in 1877 and 1878. On October 13, 1882,
Elizabeth died in childbirth along with the couple's fourth child. She
was hailed as a "model wife and mother" in her obituary. She left
her husband with three young children to raise and a large ranch
to run alone. In addition, his Civil War injuries frequently made it
difficult for him to walk.

Ratcliff sent daughters Elizabeth (Lizzy) and Lavina (Vina) to
Missouri in 1884 to live with his sisters-in-law, where the girls could

receive a proper education. He and son Howell ran the entire homestead, and Howell attended school when he could. Ten years later, the daughters, now teenagers, returned to the ranch, reuniting the family. However, their reappearance soon bought trouble through no fault of their own.

Continuing his daughters' education was important to Ratcliff, but the nearest school was seven miles from the Ratcliff ranch. Treacherous winter weather made the trip especially hard, and school was held only during three winter months. It was too far for Lizzy and Vina to walk and often dangerous to drive a horse team, even though the school was located on the Tarryall Road.

Ratcliff tried addressing the issue in several ways—from teaching his children at home to suggesting the school district institute a summer school program.

A neighbor named Mrs. Whitten reprimanded him for wanting a summer school program. She told Ratcliff that he would be waiting a long time for school to come to him. His response was ominous: "That there was something that he could do and that he would do, that he could do it and he would do it." Ratcliff wrote to Park County Superintendent of Schools George Miller to ask for free textbooks for Lizzie, Vina, and Howell, claiming that other students in the district had been supplied books.

In late summer 1894, school board member Lincoln McCurdy, a single man who had previously worked at Ratcliff's ranch, told the other board members that Lizzie Ratcliff was "six months gone" and that her father was the impregnator. It is unknown if McCurdy started the rumor himself or if he was repeating gossip. In any case, the rumor was untrue. Lizzie did not give birth to a child that fall.

The Ratcliff family was unaware of the gossip until another neighbor, Mrs. Susan Crockett, decided to inform Mr. Ratcliff by sending him the letter transcribed on the following page, dated August 22, 1894.

Mr. Ratcliff,

My letter to you is on a painful subject but I will endeavor to be as direct & brief as possible, but first let me remind you that your daughters need you to love to protect them and so do nothing rash.

Take a sensible & practical view of the situation and remember I place myself in the position of reporter simply because I think it is right you should know & were our positions reversed, I am doing to you simply as I would be done by.

McCurdy—on Lee's ranch—made the statement before the board of directors that one of your daughters—I do not know which—was six month's pregnant. Whether this originated with McCurdy or not, I do not know. I have heard that he said he heard it. This report is generally known but is not generally believed. I will refer you to a few persons that I know have heard it. Sam Lassell, Mrs. Borden, Mr. & Mrs. Sanborn, Mrs. Lapham and Mr. Crockett.

I am truly the well wisher of your family & self.

Mrs. M. Crockett.

The following spring, Ratcliff resumed his letter-writing campaign to Superintendent Miller and the school board regarding obtaining textbooks and school attendance. When matters were not addressed to his satisfaction, he sent a letter of complaint to the Superintendent of Public Instruction in Denver.

Utterly frustrated, Ratcliff decided to file a slander suit, theorizing that if he won, his children would have money for their education and living expenses upon his death. However, he decided to give the board members one last chance to admit they lied about Lizzie's condition by confronting them at the annual board meeting to be held at the schoolhouse on May 6, 1895. If McCurdy did not admit he had told the other board members a lie, and if all the members did not acknowledge it was a lie, Ratcliff reckoned he would ride to Fairplay to file the suit.

Ratcliff arrived at the schoolhouse early and went inside at 10 a.m., leaning on his cane to steady his legs and keeping his Winchester rifle by his side. Treasurer George Wyatt sat in the corner, whittling on a pencil with a pocketknife. The two made small talk until Secretary Samuel Taylor and Chairman Lincoln McCurdy came in. Superintendent Miller and E. R. Crosier were not present.

The rancher immediately stated his business—he demanded an apology or he would file a slander suit against the three. According to later testimony, no sooner was the word *suit* out of Ratcliff's mouth than Wyatt "sprang onto the floor, cracked his fist; his knife blade was sticking up here (gesturing) and swore no live man should bring him before the Court on a charge like that." Taylor and McCurdy agreed they would not tolerate a lawsuit that alleged they had repeated incest rumors.

Ratcliff later testified at his trial:

Taylor waved his left hand, put his right hand into his overalls and waved his left hand in an angry manner and he says, "Now, boys," and they came down at me at a rapid gait, and talking and hollering, you couldn't hear what they said. I begged them to stay where they were.

But they kept coming at him, and Ratcliff fired a warning shot into the floor. "Stay where you are or the next one is yours," the rancher warned, but Taylor leaped forward and Ratcliff fired. Taylor took the blast in the face, falling against a bench, then the wall, and landing face down. Dr. O.J. Mayne stated during the trial that the bullet, "entered on the left side of the face, broke the lower jaw and passed backward, coming out just about the base of the skull, about the center." Ratcliff's testimony tells what happened next:

I immediately turned to McCurdy, who came in around the end of these seats and fired at him from the seat here, all of them. And I thought I had missed the first shot and I pumped in another.

Ratcliff shot McCurdy twice in the back, both bullets lodging near the spine. Wyatt was also shot twice in the back.

Dr. Scott, a physician who arrived at the scene, was asked at the trial by prosecuting attorney Charles Wilkin what he did for Wyatt. Dr. Scott replied, "I saw he was dying. I gave him a hypodermic injection. He was suffering a good deal of pain. I told him that was all I could do for him, give him a hypodermic injection of morphine, also injections of glycerin and also whiskey."

Wyatt was able to give a statement to Dr. Scott before he died. The statement was printed, in part, in the *Rocky Mountain News*, May 8, 1895.

I was shot by Benjamin Radcliff (sic) as was also Samuel Taylor and L.F. McCurdy. No one else was armed; no blows were struck before the shooting. A heated discussion preceded the shooting. Radcliff claimed that we (Taylor, McCurdy and myself) had slandered him and said he had an intrigue with his own daughter. No attempt was made by any of the parties to assault Radcliff. Five shots were fired . . . No conversation took place after the first shot was fired.

After the shootings, Ratcliff left the schoolhouse and mounted up to ride into Fairplay to turn himself in to the sheriff for killing the school board members. Word of the shootings soon spread. One miner at the scene hitched up Wyatt's team and drove into Como to fetch Dr. Scott while others tried to locate Deputy Sheriff James Link in Como. When Mrs. Wyatt learned what had happened, she ran screaming down the road toward her home.

Two separate scenarios emerged: the crisis at the schoolhouse and the arrest of Ratcliff. The scene at the schoolhouse intensified as more and more people arrived to offer help. At one point, a dozen people were in and out of the unsecured crime scene. When Dr. Scott arrived, he straightened the bodies to determine the bullets' points of entry and to search the deceased for weapons. The only weapon found was Wyatt's pocketknife.

The bodies could not be removed from the building until the county coroner, Dr. Mayne of Como, held an inquest, which was legally mandated when there was a death by unlawful or unknown means. In addition, the inquest results had to be kept secret until a suspect was arrested if unlawful or felonious intent was determined.

Some said the coroner's panel was stacked against Ratcliff. Of the six people Dr. Mayne summoned, three were nearby placer mine owners and three were Tarryall-area ranchers, including Charles Dunbar, with whom Ratcliff had a previous legal conflict. On the other hand, it would have taken time to serve summonses to folks in the outlying towns or ranches, which would have required the bodies to lay much longer thereby causing even more distress for the family members and allowing time for someone to tamper with the evidence.

As it were, the coroner's inquest did not convene until 9 p.m. the night of the murders, and was held outside the schoolhouse. Dr. Mayne made it clear: "We are not trying the case, we are here only to determine the cause of death," according to the *Rocky Mountain News* of May 7, 1895. In the same article, the newspaper opined, "The jury viewed the sickening sight last night, made more ghastly by the light of flickering candles." A dozen witnesses to Ratcliff's presence in the vicinity that day stood by in the cool evening air, eager to testify. When the inquiry terminated late that evening, Taylor's family claimed his body and took it home. Wyatt and McCurdy still lay where they fell.

All this standing around was not doing Ratcliff's neck any good, for talk soon turned to how to take care of the matter of punishment quickly and without the court's purview. Newspaper accounts of the scene when the coroner's panel reconvened the next morning, added fuel to the fire. The *Rocky Mountain News* described the scene in a front page article:

> Those who came early in the day found two stiff and cold bodies lying on the floor of the uncouth log school house,

one surrounded by a pool of thick blood, the other on a
coarse mattress, and over the corpse was the swaying body
of a woman, distracted by grief, and moaning piteously for
one spark of life in the cold, staring eyes, while huddled in a
corner, shuddering with a fear they could not understand,
was a group of children who wondered between their sobs,
whether the cold, bloody form was the father they had
romped with and who yesterday kissed them good-bye.

The bodies remained in the schoolhouse until noon, awaiting
the panel's findings. Crowds came to peer in the windows and
traipse around the school property. The panel finally reached its
conclusions, stating: "We find that L. F. McCurdy, Sam'l Taylor and
G. D. Wyatt came to their deaths from gun shot wounds from a gun
in the hands of Benjamin Radcliff & that the shooting was done with
felonious intent." McCurdy's and Wyatt's bodies were released to
their families, and both were buried in the Como cemetery. Taylor
was initially laid to rest in the Bordenville Cemetery; but the
remains were disinterred and reburied in Denver's Fairmount
Cemetery on October 31, 1902.

Meanwhile, a second scenario was playing out as Ratcliff rode
toward Fairplay. Deputy Sheriff Link had already been informed of
the murders and rode out to intercept Ratcliff. The two, who had
known each other for years, met up a half mile east of Como
around noon the day of the shootings.

"Which way you headed?" inquired Link.

"Fairplay," Ratcliff responded.

"Then I will accompany you," said the deputy, and he allowed
Ratcliff to ride on a little ahead of him. Link and Ratcliff had been
on friendly terms, but on this ride the conversation was mostly official business. The two stopped in Como, where Ratcliff willingly surrendered his arms. Link hitched up a team and drove the suspect by
wagon toward the county seat. They soon came upon Sheriff Daniel
Wilson, who took charge of the prisoner, and Link accompanied
them into Fairplay. On the trip, Ratcliff fully acknowledged that he
had killed the three men because "they all made a rush at him."

When the trio arrived at the county jail, the sheriff took possession of the weapons confiscated by Link. Wilson's detailed inventory

included the Winchester rifle containing fourteen shots in the magazine and one in the barrel; twenty-seven rifle cartridges; and a six-shooter revolver with six cartridges, for a total of forty-eight available shots. Granted, it was common knowledge around those parts that Ratcliff always traveled armed because he feared retaliation by his neighbors for making his lawsuit intentions known and worried about being ambushed on the road. That day, however, he carried an excessive amount of firepower.

Offering the prisoner his arm to steady his walk, Wilson ushered Benjamin Ratcliff into an awaiting cell. Wilson later testified that Ratcliff was not excitable and was a model prisoner: "First rate—good a prisoner as I ever had." However, Ratcliff did not stay long in Park County.

Rumors reached Governor Albert McIntyre's office that outraged Park County citizens planned to lock Ratcliff in the school building and set it on fire to avenge his victims. Not wanting a repeat of the 1880 lynchings of William Porter and John Hoover, Sheriff Wilson and a deputy drove Ratcliff to the Chaffee County jail in Buena Vista in the dead of night.

When a large crowd arrived at the Fairplay jail the next morning to get a glimpse of the murderer, they were disappointed to learn that he was gone—in fact, they did not believe the guards until they were allowed to look through the jail cells. The May 8, 1895, edition of the *Denver Evening Post* was quick to applaud the move.

This is well. It is better that he should be legally punished. His punishment should be quick and the full limit of the law. The case is a good one on which to commence that severity and promptness of punishment which will serve as an effective warning against murder and make life and the happiness of families a little safer.

That same issue of the newspaper republished a Buena Vista article that commented on Ratcliff's move:

A large guard has been placed around the jail and will resist any mob that might come down to lynch the prisoner. He is closely guarded and no one is allowed to see or speak with him. Every precaution is being taken by the authorities to prevent any trouble.

The article's caption, "Safe in Jail," was a misnomer because another report soon reached the governor. This one claimed that 100 men planned to take the train from Como to Buena Vista, storm the jail, and hang the suspect. The scene of gawkers thronging the Fairplay jail was repeated in Buena Vista twenty-four hours later.

Terse telegrams questioning the security of Buena Vista's calaboose were exchanged between the governor and Chaffee County Sheriff Joseph Gallup. When McIntyre asked how secure the Chaffee County jail was, Gallup replied:

> There is intense feeling in Park County against Radcliff. Perhaps he would be safer if he was farther away from the scene of the trouble. We have a good jail, but do not know how many men would be willing to make a fight in his behalf.

Governor McIntyre asked that the prisoner be moved to the Pueblo County jail, to which Pueblo Sheriff Arthur Moses responded, "[I] will do everything I can."

It had been a long day for Ratcliff when he arrived at the Pueblo County jail at 2:30 a.m. on May 8, 1895, after undergoing two moves in two days to protect him from mob violence. He remained there until his trial date two months later, although at some point he was again jailed in Fairplay for three weeks. Given the furor brought about by the defendant's alleged crimes in Park County, the trial was moved to the Buena Vista Courthouse in Chaffee County.

Court was called to order on July 15, 1895, with the Honorable Morton S. Bailey presiding. Bailey was the district judge of the Eleventh Judicial District, which included Chaffee, Custer, Fremont, and Park Counties. He was also a former Park County resident and attorney there for many years. This left some to wonder if the jurisdiction switch was even worth it.

The first order of business was to decide if the defendant should be tried separately for each murder count with three separate juries or by one jury for all three. The court ruled that Ratcliff would be tried for all three murders by the same jury.

The three Ratcliff children, now 20, 18, and 17, sat in the courtroom close to their father. Lizzie and Vina wore heavy veils. Ratcliff held his hand cupped to his left ear to aid his hearing. Attorney and former circuit court judge Vinton G. Holliday represented the accused, with assistance from the defendant himself. The defense was partially based on the school board's response to the defendant's threat of lawsuit and his "fits of temporary insanity." Ratcliff himself maintained that his motive was self-defense.

On July 20, 1895, lead prosecuting attorney George Hartenstein closed by orating the State's case for two hours. Mrs. Wyatt burst into tears and had to leave the courtroom. Defense attorney Holliday likewise presented an impassioned plea for leniency. Five hours later, the jury reached its decision: guilty of first-degree murder on all three counts.

Holliday immediately rose and asked for five days to file for a new trial, which was granted. The *Rocky Mountain News* reported, "Radcliff was the coolest man in the crowded court room." As he did throughout the trial, Ratcliff listened intently as the court imposed the lethal sentence, all the while stroking his long beard and occasionally using a spittoon.

Four days later, Benjamin Ratcliff was returned to the courtroom to hear his fate, a fate he already knew because first-degree murder carried a mandatory death sentence. Turning to the defen-

Benjamin Ratcliff was executed by the state in 1896, one of only two residents of the county to meet such a fate. *Courtesy Colorado State Archives*

dant, Judge Bailey asked: "Have you anything to say why sentence should not be pronounced?" Ratcliff answered: "I am an innocent man; if the sentence is a just one I have no objection at all to it."

He was sentenced to be hanged at the Colorado State Penitentiary the week of August 11, 1895. Ratcliff kissed his daughters and was whisked off to jail to await transport to the penitentiary that evening.

With only five days to file a writ of supersedeas, which would at least temporarily prevent the Chaffee County Court from imposing the death penalty, Holliday dashed off to the Colorado Supreme Court in Denver, only to discover that the court papers had not been transcribed and remained with a Buena Vista stenographer. The documents arrived in Denver days later, and Holliday filed the writ motion on August 7, 1895.

The substance of Holliday's request for the writ was that the trial court erred on seventeen different counts, from passing an illegal sentence to violating the defendant's constitutional rights. Holliday presented his oral argument before the Supreme Court on September 18, 1895. All defense motions were denied, and the lower court's decision was upheld.

The only other recourse was a governor's reprieve, which Holliday vigorously pursued. Ratcliff was allowed to submit a handwritten request himself, which one newspaper scoffed at and called "foolscap."

The newly established Board of Pardons called a special session, because Ratcliff's execution date was scheduled prior to the board's next meeting. Holliday made a personal plea to Governor McIntyre, claiming his client had a strong basis for an insanity plea. The board immediately sent letters to Judge Bailey, the jury members, the attorneys, and some trial witnesses to attend the special session, which was called to order on February 5, 1896, at 8 p.m. In an effort to pursue a final line of defense, Holliday, now assisted by former Park County attorney M. J. Bartley, brought up a "heat of passion" defense, hoping to raise doubt in the board members' minds that Ratcliff was sane at the time, even though the Supreme Court had disallowed this argument. Holliday did not mince words in this last-ditch effort to save his client from the awaiting gallows. "I was hand-icapped by the insane cunning, bent with all its trickery to beat me," said the judge in the February 6, 1896 issue of the *Rocky Mountain*

News. Blaming his inability to properly defend his client on Ratcliff himself, he continued,

He (Ratcliff) was determined that I should not plead insanity and he bent all his crazy cunning to deceive the doctors in the examination and the court and jury later. The plea of self-defense was the only one that Radcliff would consent to. Nevertheless, a stout deputy sheriff was seated close behind him every moment that he was in the court room, showing that the court feared an outbreak at any time.

Some of Ratcliff's old acquaintances spoke on their friend's behalf, describing his occasional odd behaviors. Mrs. Carrie O. Kistler, who taught in Ratcliff's school district in the early 1880s, also submitted comments regarding Ratcliff's "flashes of madness." The intent was to obtain their friend's earthly salvation, not to demean him. On the other side, a number of Michigan Creek ranch residents attended and spoke against a reprieve.

One final visitor appeared at the governor's office. Mr. O. P. Wallack, with whom Ratcliff had spoken regarding filing a slander suit, was one of the first men at the crime scene. Wallack asked to witness the hanging at the request of victims' families. Warden John Cleghorn denied the request, stating he didn't want to issue any more tickets to "the show." One reason the State had taken jurisdiction over executions was to remove the "carnival-like atmosphere" that prevailed at the county hangings.

After all the impassioned speeches, the board unanimously voted against a sentence commutation. Execution was set between February 6 and 8, 1896. Ratcliff was moved to the penitentiary's "condemned" cell in the execution wing, and placed on death watch. He remained stoic throughout the wait.

What did a death watch mean? A January 13, 1892, *Rocky Mountain News* article educated the public in graphic detail:

The death watch means that not only is there a man outside the door, but there is another inside, who sets upon a low stool, faces the prisoner and is under obligation never to remove his eyes, so that a moment's motion to swallow poison, though lightning-like in its rapidity, would not succeed in evading the vigilance of the inexorable law, which orders that the condemned shall be hanged by the neck until dead. . . .

BEFORE THE PARDON BOARD.

Attorney M. J. Bartley argued for his client's life before the Board of Pardons on February 5, 1896. The drawing appeared in the *Rocky Mountain News* the following day.

Even before the death watch is established, the outer guard is required to communicate every half hour during the night with the captain of the guard. There is a perfect system of electric signals for all purposes.

The execution time was at the prison official's discretion; custom dictated execution would occur at night on the slim chance that the Supreme Court of the United States intervened the very day of execution. The executioner was John J. "Jack" Eeles, a longtime prison employee who was killed in a prison riot in 1929.

The original 1896 wording in the *Rocky Mountain News* edition of February 8, 1896, best captures the suspense of the murderer's final moments:

Radcliff was sitting quietly in his cell at 7:40 when the witnesses required by law to be present at the hanging, filed in to the corridor and made their way by his cell door to the room in which he was to give up his life for the three he had taken last May. The condemned man scarcely noticed them. The witnesses all took their place and then the warden, accompanied by a deputy and the chaplain, approached the cell occupied by the prisoner. ...Then the warden led the way to the room in which the gallows was stationed, Radcliff followed quietly. Entering the brilliantly lighted room, he glanced about him at the various witnesses.

Radcliff was pinioned, the black cap drawn over his head and the noose adjusted, and all present watched the dial that indicated when the weight was to fall. Radcliff's neck was broken by the twitch-up. Fifteen minutes afterward, the body was cut down and the attending physicians state that death was instantaneous.

Local newspapers reported that because of the train schedule, Ratcliff's remains laid at the Buena Vista train station for two days before they were shipped back to Como.

Thus ended the saga of Park County's only triple homicide of the nineteenth-century. Many questions remain. Was Ratcliff a disabled old man who was bullied into violence by other ranchers because of his eccentricities? And when the bullying turned on one of his children, did he do as many protective fathers would and overreact to the insult on their honor? Or did he plan to murder the school board members when he learned they would be together for the annual meeting?

On a barren, isolated hilltop, under a small grave marker bearing no acknowledgment of his heroic Civil War service, lie all the answers to Benjamin Ratcliff's behavior on the day of May 6, 1895.

THE MURDER SITE TODAY

The Michigan Creek school house is gone but was located approximately six miles east of Jefferson on the Tarryall Road.

THE RATCLIFF HOMESTEAD

The homestead is on U.S. Forest Service land. Stop in at the Forest Service office at the junction of Highway 285 and Main Street in Fairplay for specific directions and to gain permission to access the site.

Puma City in its heyday, 1898. *Courtesy Park County Local History Archives*
Source: U.S. Geological Survey.

Chapter Fifteen

SALOON SHOOTING in PUMA CITY
1897

Near the turn of the century, minerals were discovered in the Puma Hills area of the Tarryall River valley. These hills are well named. The rocky outcrops provide a perfect environment for the puma, or mountain lion. The valley is in contrast to the South Park Basin both in geology and appearance. The basin is low and broad, with rolling hills, while the Puma Hills are a deep reddish color, with jagged hillsides.

The town of Puma City, located closer to Lake George than Jefferson on County Road 77, was created in the early spring of 1896 after the Gilmore brothers and George A. Starbird from Victor, Colorado, came north, prospecting along the way. The group soon found gold, silver, copper, and other minerals and started the mining settlement. By December of that year, A. G. Hartman from the U.S. Surveyor General's Office in Washington, D.C., had surveyed properties to ensure that the town site and the mining claims were properly aligned to avoid any confusion later. There were twenty businesses or residences plus many tents and approximately 100 men prospecting in the hills. The most productive mines were the Boomer and the June.

The number of buildings soon doubled. The Midland railroad station in Lake George was a jumping-off point for passengers to catch the four-horse stagecoach to Puma—a thirteen-mile journey that took more than two hours. Those coming from Denver had a five-hour stage ride from Jefferson, forty-five miles away.

To provide the new camp's liquid refreshments, the county initially issued two liquor licenses, the first one on December 10, 1896, to Peter S. Cox, owner of the Long Branch saloon. The other license went to partners Becker and Kleinknecht on December 30, 1896. No doubt business was booming right along with mines. To try to keep a lid on the wild spirits springing forth nightly from the drinking establishments, M. S. Robinson was appointed justice of the peace on January 15, 1897. Similar to the situation in Hall Valley in the 1870s, Puma City was far from the county seat and the county sheriff. This made it hard to control the rowdiness, especially since Robinson was not a very effective justice of the peace.

Pete Cox, or "Mexican Pete" as he was generally known, moved to Puma City from Enid, Oklahoma. He was part Mexican, which did not endear him to his fellow miners and businessmen in those days. Citizens had recently run a Chinese man out of Puma City for trying to set up a laundry, even though this type of Chinese business was common in Fairplay. In addition to owning the Long Branch saloon, Cox also owned and operated a meat market and eating house. He also had mining interests via a partnership with W. G. Williams of Mancos, Colorado, and Mrs. Ida Lambert of Puma City, but the names of the specific mines are unknown.

On March 3, 1897, Cox and James R. Gregg—who also owned a saloon in partnership with Charles Combs of Grant (see Chapter 3)— had a run-in in the new town of Jasper City, a few miles southeast of Puma City. The *Fairplay Flume* reported that Cox was in the process of buying Gregg's establishment, although it is unclear whether the business was located in Jasper City or in Puma City. Cox claimed that Gregg agreed not to open a competing business and to leave town, but in fact, Gregg opened a new saloon almost across the street.

On March 4, 1897, the *Denver Evening Post* reported that Gregg had shot and killed a Denver con man who was running a "shell game" in a saloon. Gregg had intervened during an altercation between the con man and another saloon patron. Gregg was eventually acquitted on a plea of self-defense. He was reputed to have killed at least three men in saloon fights in his hometown of Enid, Oklahoma, according to the same newspaper account.

Stories recounting Cox's death differ, typical of many murder scenarios. The following accounts of the evening's events are cobbled together from eyewitnesses and newspaper accounts.

Pete Cox was very agitated over Gregg's backing out of the saloon deal. Cox had a strange look on his face when he went into the Puma City Dance Hall the night of the murder carrying his Winchester rifle. One of his friends pulled him aside and asked, "Pete, are you hunting trouble this evening?"

"I am not," he replied tersely, then proceeded to tell his friend how Gregg insulted him earlier that day in Jasper over the saloon sale. Another friend, W. W. Freeman, advised him to go home, saying, "It looks like there will be trouble here."

"I will not go a damn step," Cox retorted. "There can be no damn son-of-a-bitch to abuse me and make me rub."

Cox then stepped behind the bar as Gregg came up. Gregg asked Charlie Harrison (the day bartender) and J. W. Fulton to take a drink. Seeing Cox standing behind the bar, Gregg launched into a tirade of name-calling directed at Cox, including calling him a "half-breed." Cox backed up against a mirror, raised his left hand, and said, "I don't want any bother here." Others testified that Cox told Gregg, "Stand back and don't you follow me."

Cox moved toward the other end of the bar and raised his rifle shoulder high, as if he was going to shoot. No doubt the air was heavy with suspense and dread by this time. "Hold on," yelled Gregg. A shot rang out! "Jack" Rumsey, the bartender, later identified the shooter as Charles Harrison, known as the "Aspen Kid." Men scurried for cover, some hiding behind the icebox next to the back bar.

One witness reported that after two more shots were fired, Gregg dropped to the floor, shouting: "Boys, where are your guns?" His cohorts quickly responded, and "bullets flew fast," clogging the air with so much gun smoke that the damage could not be seen until the dust settled.

A *Rocky Mountain News* reporter noted on March 5, 1897:

Gregg received a ball that plowed three or four inches of his left shoulder from his coat and a little graze on his right groin. Another smaller-sized bullet went through the left skirt of his hip coat. . . . Harrison's right eye was injured by the shots, so close were they fired. . . . James "Jack" Rumsey, the bartender, had the corner of a black hat he wore shot off.

The *Denver Post* correspondent said in his March 4, 1897, column: "Your correspondent saw Gregg put the gun in Cox's breast and fire while two of Gregg's friends held him. Afterward, while Cox was trying to get up in the door, Gregg fired two more shots at him."

The mayor of West Cripple Creek, Charles H. Lewis, was present and provided very detailed information to the coroner's inquest panel, stating Cox was the one who filled Gregg's coat full of bullet holes. Dr. Hayes's medical testimony was that two bullets penetrated the body from in front and one from the back, the latter causing death. The panel brought in the following verdict:

> We, the jury, find that P.S. Cox came to his death from gun-shot wounds at the hands of one James R. Gregg and the man known as the "Aspen Kid," alias Charles Harrison. We, the jury, are unable to decide whether this killing was done feloniously or not.

Gregg's coat was retained for evidence. He wore the holey thing into Fairplay one month later, on April 2, promptly winning the *Flume's* favorable comments in the April 4, 1897, issue: "It is very evident he did not do all of the shooting. If that is not coming all around a man and putting him in a close corner, we don't know what is."

Other evidence was botched by Justice of the Peace Robinson, who was reportedly taking advice from Gregg's attorney, Mr. Weymouth. Weymouth had taken Gregg and two of his companions (Charles Combs and "Long John") into his own home. Robinson did not arrest anyone—the arrests did not come for another three days, when the coroner placed two pistols and Cox's Winchester into evidence and set bond. Additionally, the body was not properly handled after it was taken to a house (presumably to Cox's house). On March 5, 1897, the *Rocky Mountain News* wrote:

> Cox's body was stripped after its removal to the house, the clothing worn at the time of the shooting taken off and thrown away. . . . Justice of the Peace Robinson removed the body from where it lay after the killing a day before the arrival of the coroner and undoubtedly some matters important in evidence were removed by others.

The murder caused a lot of excitement in town for the next few days, until Sheriff Daniel Wilson arrived to settle things down. The Denver papers picked up on the agitation, stating:

> Friends of both parties, who are mostly of the saloon and gambling fraternity, are making it warm for each other and in fact, everyone else, by threats, etc. not even sparing newspaper men whom they threatened if their reports were unfavorable.

The *Rocky Mountain News* of March 8, 1897, scolded: "There appears to be necessity for better organization of civil government in the new mining camp for Puma City. There can be no permanent progress without security to life and property." Another article in the *Denver Evening Post* on March 9 titled, "Has Ores and Toughs," claimed that an attempt was made to elect a marshal recently but was defeated by the "dance hall element."

These dangerous conditions were not lost on the law in Fairplay. One week after the shootings, Sheriff Wilson appointed J. W. Diamond and J. H. Drifuse deputies at Puma City. They were described as "straight-forward, fearless citizens and will do their duty," in the Flume's March 12, 1897, edition. Wilson spent a few days in the camp to set everyone straight on the law's function, straight on the law's function and that it applied equally to all, not just to those living in Fairplay.

Despite the coroner's inconclusive ruling, both Gregg and Harrison were arrested because of the incriminating testimony. Rumsey captured Harrison in Florissant the next day, a daring move on his part. Gregg was held under $5,000 bond, while Harrison's was set at $500, with both to appear at the District Court trial in Fairplay in May 1897. Gregg was able to post bond immediately, but the Aspen Kid was unable to come up with bondsmen willing to guarantee his future appearance.

Everything was geared up for a May 2 trial: Ray McLaughlin, a well-known local rancher, brought a wagonload of witnesses into town. Other citizens traveled to the county seat on their own, filling up the town. Then a small notice appeared in the paper that the trial might not be held in May, even after more than forty witnesses were subpoenaed. The reason was that another murder trial was occupying the court's time: that of Oscar Stringham, a friend of Gregg's (see Chapter 1).

At the end of June, Gregg's attorney, C. A. Wilkin, was able to get Gregg's bond reduced from $5,000 down to $3,000; likewise, Harrison's was also reduced. The murder trial was finally held on October 22, 1897. All charges against both suspects were dismissed. That same day, the local newspaper summarized the trial and seemed to fix the blame on the victim.

> In the case of the people vs. J.R. Gregg, which has been on trial this week, the jury found the defendant, who was charged with the murder of a half-breed Indian named Pete Cox at Puma City last March, not guilty. The verdict gives general satisfaction, as the deceased, according to the evidence, was a "bad man" from Oklahoma, who spent most of his time itching for someone to kill. On the night last March, when he took his change of venue he went to the dance hall in Puma, armed with a Winchester with the avowed purpose of killing Gregg, but after firing two shots, both of which pierced Gregg's clothing, he was killed himself.

The paper went on to poke fun at the state's evidence, given by the men who hid behind the icebox the night of the murder and supposedly watched the entire crime unfold.

> The State's only evidence was given by what is known as the "Ice Box Brigade," a detachment of the Puma Light Artillery, Capt. J. Wind Barnes commanding. They received their title from the fact that they were able to see all of the proceedings through six feet of icebox, behind which they were crouched and through the clouds of smoke from numerous guns. After the trial, these Don Quixotes furnished much amusement by their crest-fallen manner in which they retreated from the scene of the fray which turned out so differently from the way they had hoped. This is the only military organization extant whose members are trained to watch a bullet in its flight.

Harrison was warmly received back into the community and even "got up" a dance in Alma with the Fairplay orchestra playing the very next week.

Peter Cox was laid to rest in the Lake George Cemetery. A stone marker was installed in the spring of 2012 by the cemetery committee, headed by longtime Tarryall resident Steven Plutt, who has held community fund-raisers to purchase headstones for those long departed.

PUMA CITY SITE TODAY

Puma City still stands in the form of a few dilapidated wood buildings between Jefferson and Lake George on County Road 77, the Tarryall Road, thirteen miles from Lake George and thirty miles from Jefferson. The buildings are now on private property but are quite visible from the road. Trespassing is prohibited.

John Peoples refused to testify against his coworkers James Brady and John
Williams. All were suspects in the murder of Cosmino Granitti. A close look at
Peoples' mug shot shows a tear in his left eye. *Courtesy Colorado State Archives*

Chapter Sixteen

ELEVEN MILE CANYON CAPER
1886

In the summer of 1885, construction began on the Colorado Midland Railway, needed as a means to haul lumber and other supplies up and down Ute Pass and over into the Leadville area. Track was first laid from Leadville to Aspen, then construction began into South Park, with track traveling via Granite Canyon, now called Eleven Mile Canyon or Park County Road 96.

One of the railroad construction camps was called Bradbury, located at the mouth of Eleven Mile Canyon near Lake George. A young man named John "Jack" Peoples was part of the "scraper gang," whose job was to dig up the soil for the railroad bed. In the West, the popular Fresno drag scraper was often used, a large metal "scooper" operated by one man driving a horse team. A four-horse scraper measured five feet by eighteen inches; smaller versions were made for two and three-horse teams. The average speed was two hundred feet per minute because the scraper had to be dumped frequently.

On the night of August 24, 1886, the gang's foreman, Edmond W. Hamlin, awakened around midnight when he heard shots fired close by. Hamlin then heard a man being beaten—hollering and begging his assailant to stop.

Hamlin kept a watchful eye on the other tents. Thirty minutes later, he saw John Williams and Jack Peoples coming out of the cook tent. Hamlin met up with them and asked, "Where are you going?"

Peoples spoke up, "I'm going to kill all the damned dagoes!" He complained that one of the Italian laborers had hit him earlier that day.

Hamlin saw a Colt revolver in his hand and asked, "Where are you going with that gun?" and grabbed it.

Peoples responded by drawing a knife on his boss, threatening: "Let go of my pistol or I will kill you!" Hamlin immediately complied.

Peoples then walked around the Italians' tent, and when he was thirty feet away, he fired five shots through the canvas. Hamlin grabbed him, saying, "Stop! You probably hurt someone!"

With that, Peoples drew a second short pistol, cocked it, and stuck it in the Hamlin's face, with the warning, "If you don't let go, I will kill you."

Again Hamlin released his grip, and Peoples walked away but soon returned.

Hamlin checked the tent that Peoples had fired into and discovered one man dead. The *Leadville Herald Times* identified the victim as Cosmino Granitti. A second laborer, Antonia Gancola, was wounded.

When coworker James Brady saw the carnage in the tent, he said to Peoples, "See what you have done?"

Peoples replied, "Brady, I did not do all this."

"Shut up or I will kill you," Brady retorted.

Fairplay physician J. B. Beers arrived to treat Gancola, noting a gunshot wound in the left shoulder; however, he was not able to extricate the bullet. Gancola initially improved, but four days later, lockjaw set in. Dr. Beers testified that upon his final visit to the patient:

> As soon as I entered the room I saw that he was dying. He had lockjaw at that time. He could not speak or swallow and his jaws were set. The muscles of the jaw were knotted. My opinion is that he died from the effect of the gunshot wound in the left shoulder.

Williams and Brady took off from the camp heading south, afraid their association with Peoples would implicate them in the murder. Brady may have been even more involved according to the September 3, 1886, *Leadville Herald Democrat*. The newspaper reported that witnesses saw Brady with a smoking gun in his hand right after Peoples fired into the tent, implying that Brady's shot may have hit one of the victims. Although Williams' involvement is unclear, the fact that he was associated with Peoples and Brady may have been cause enough for him to run. Peoples was apprehended in the Bradbury vicinity on Saturday night, August 28, by a man in his sixties, who delivered the suspect to the sheriff.

The Park County commissioners offered a reward on October 8, 1886, as did Governor Benjamin Eaton, for the capture and return of Brady and Williams to the Park County's sheriff. The reward money totaled $300 for Brady and $400 for his sidekick. With a price on their heads, the two outlaws were apprehended in Gunnison County, Colorado, by well-known Sheriff C. W. "Doc" Shores, although the exact time frame is unknown.

Peoples' trial was held first. He was convicted of accessory to murder, and received a three-year prison in October 1886.

Brady's and Williams' trials came up two years later, in April 1888. Peoples was brought from the penitentiary to the Fairplay courtroom to testify against them, but he refused to do so, believing his life was on the line if he did.

Jack Peoples' testimony might have made a difference. Brady was found not guilty after the jury deliberated for only twenty minutes. With this swift acquittal, the district attorney decided to dismiss all charges against Williams, assuming he could not win that case either. The co-defendants walked out of the courtroom, and Brady even attended a dance in Fairplay that night. The *Fairplay Flume* was not happy with the trial's cost of $3,000 and the prosecution's lack of effort against Williams.

Jack Peoples was released from prison on April 26, 1889. A small undated handwritten notation on his prison record simply states, "Escaped," but there are no details as to when this happened or when he was recaptured.

THE MURDER SITE TODAY

Eleven Mile Canyon is managed by the U. S. Forest Service. The popular spot for camping, fishing and other recreation is on County Road 96, a gravel road that is the former railroad bed.

Turn south from State Highway 24 in Lake George and drive approximately one mile, then veer right to continue on County Road 96.

The scenic route follows the South Platte River, providing views of the rushing water below and mountain vistas. The road goes through three tunnels with cinder residue still visible on the ceilings. The road ends at Eleven Mile State Park.

The Espinosas brothers' first Park County victim, John Addleman, is buried in a small cemetery near Lake George. *Courtesy Christie Wright*

Chapter Seventeen

THE INFAMOUS ESPINOSAS
1863

The early 1860s were a traumatic time for South Park residents. The Civil War called men away in 1861 shortly after the mining craze took hold. In 1863, two brothers, Jim and John Reynolds, Hamilton-area prospectors and Confederate sympathizers, began robbing South Park way stops and stagecoaches to obtain money to further their cause—the Confederate takeover of Colorado. Although the Reynolds brothers never killed anyone in these efforts, they terrified many citizens along the way.

After carving a path of lawlessness through Park County, the Reynolds boys and their cohorts were captured and killed east of Denver at Russellville by soldiers under the orders of the notorious Colonel John Chivington. The following year, 1864, began what was dubbed the "Reign of Terror" by another set of brothers, Felipe Niero and Jose Vivian Espinosa, who lived in the San Luis Valley near present-day Antonito, Colorado.

Much has been written about the duo, and several different accounts of their lives and actions exist. According to the New Mexico state historian's website, Felipe and Vivian Espinosa were sons of Pedro Ygnacio Espinosa and Maria Gertrudis Chavez. Felipe was born around 1832, and Vivian a few years later. The family lived in the small town of El Rito, north of Taos. In 1847, when Felipe was a teenager, the "Taos Revolt" took place during the Mexican-American War. This was basically a land dispute wherein the Hispanic land owners were promised titles to their property that would be recognized and honored by the United States, but they ended up losing land instead. In addition, the occupying American soldiers under Colonel Sterling Price were extremely disrespectful to the area inhabitants, thus fostering even more resentment. The Espinosas were one of many families who lost their land.

Felipe looked for another source of income and turned to stealing horses. He recruited Vivian in this endeavor, and they quickly progressed to robbing freight wagons. A local priest reported their thefts, leading a Santa Fe official to contact the commanding officer at Fort Garland to arrest the two men if seen.

Eventually, an attempt was made to capture the brothers by tricking them into joining a sham military unit. The plan failed, and the brothers killed an officer of a military group that had come to their home as part of the ruse. The soldiers raided the Espinosas' home, leaving the family with literally nothing. After obtaining help and food for their families from neighbors, the entire family left their home and moved north to the San Luis Valley in 1858. The brothers absconded to the Cañon City area.

On March 16, 1863, the Espinosa brothers came upon a sawmill belonging to Franklin W. Bruce, age fifty-eight, on Hardscrabble Creek near Cañon City. The brothers shot Bruce through the heart and carved a cross into his chest. They ransacked the sawmill building before they took off.

Henry Harkens was killed two days later near the sawmill he had started with two friends, Murdock McPherson and a Mr. Bassett. The three families had recently settled in the area south of present-day Fort Carson. On March 18, McPherson and Bassett worked at the mill, leaving Harkens to put the finishing touches on his new log cabin. When the friends left the sawmill around dinnertime and walked back to Harkens cabin, they found him dead on the floor, a bullet in his forehead, a vicious axe wound to the head, and two cuts on his torso. The cabin had been ransacked.

The men dashed to a nearby ranch to warn of what they assumed was an attack by Indians. The next day, a tracking party was organized and the killers were tracked north to Colorado City, Colorado Territory's first capitol (now a National Historic District called Old Colorado City on the west side of Colorado Springs).

The brothers eluded their trackers. A week and a half later, John Addleman, a young rancher living south of Wilkerson Pass, was their first Park County victim. Addleman was found murdered in a fashion similar to the murders of Bruce and Harkens. According to Irving Howbert in his book, *Memories of a Lifetime in the Pikes Peak Region*, Addleman came from Pennsylvania. He had first settled in Colorado City before deciding to take up ranching in Park County. On March 30, 1863, a mail carrier named Mr. Rowe stopped at Addleman's on his route but did not see the rancher. Fearing marauders were nearby, he retreated, but was pursued by an unknown man. Rowe was able to lose the stranger and reported the incident in Fairplay later that evening.

A sheriff's posse rode out to Addleman's the next day to check on the young rancher. They found him dead from two gunshot wounds to the chest and his body mutilated. This was now the Espinosas' calling card—death by gunshot and mutilation of the body. Addleman was buried in a beautiful valley along County Road 90 in an area later known as Rocky; a recently erected wood sign marks his final repose.

The marauders must have liked the vantage point of high passes, because one week later, they struck near Kenosha Hill, or Kenosha Pass. Jacob Marion Binkley had come to Colorado from Iowa with his older brother John Alexander Binkley. The 1860 federal census notes the two, ages twenty and twenty-two, respectively, worked as laborers in Fairplay. On April 7, 1863, Jacob Binkley and a companion, Abraham Nelson Shoup, started out for Denver and its nearby mining regions. Shoup was the brother of Colonel George Laird Shoup, head of the Third Colorado Cavalry, which he commanded in the 1864 Sand Creek Massacre.

The next day, Binkley and Shoup drove their wagon past the Kenosha House, a popular boardinghouse, and camped one and a half miles below, along the river. Passersby observed, "They appeared to be very much elated with the prospect before them," a *Rocky Mountain News* article reported April 16, 1863.

On the morning of April 9, proprietors of the Kenosha House found Binkley, lying face down, dead. He had been shot through the chest, like the previous victims. The perpetrators had cleaned out his pockets. Shoup's body was also found, "having been stabbed three times in the chest and horribly mutilated about the head. He was lying nearly four hundred yards from the wagon, having undoubtedly made a desperate effort to escape, but in vain. He was also robbed." (This description was according to a letter from R. Berry to the *Rocky Mountain News*, dated April 16, 1863.) The two bodies were taken to Fairplay and buried in a small cemetery at the west end of town.

On April 15, 1863, soldiers from Denver, commanded by Lieutenants Luther Wilson and John Oster Jr., were sent into the Park to protect the populace and try to find the murderers. A *Weekly Commonwealth* reporter was contacted by Lt. Wilson himself, who described their mission as accompanying the mails and honoring escort requests from citizens. Some soldiers were riding fifty miles a day in their hunt for the "demonic miscreants." Although the troops did round up some "no-goods," the actual killers evaded detection. Adding insult to injury and right under the noses of the military men, the brothers struck again ten days later on a well-traveled road a few miles west of Fairplay.

On April 25, 1863, a Mr. Metcalf loaded up a wagon of timber in the thriving town of Montgomery City, located at the base of Mount Lincoln. The discovery of silver on Mount Lincoln and adjoining Mount Cameron and Mount Bross, three years earlier, made for prosperous times.. The town now lies under the Montgomery Reservoir, owned by the City of Colorado Springs. During the height of the Espinosa frenzy, young Wilbur F. Stone, who later became a Colorado Supreme Court Justice, lived and mined in Montgomery, a mining camp that now lies under Montgomery Reservoir. From there, Stone penned periodic letters to various Colorado newspapers, primarily the *Weekly Commonwealth* and the *Weekly Register Call* and occasionally the *Rocky Mountain News*, under the pen name "Dornick," meaning a pebble or stone. The young lawyer and promising writer offered rousing accounts of mountain life, often interweaving his personal opinions.

According to Stone's account, Metcalf was headed for Fairplay with his ox team when he came upon a gentleman named Bill Carter traveling on foot from the Mosquito Mining District several gulches over.

As Carter walked near the wagon, a shot rang out, felling him dead in his tracks, the bullet piercing his breast. Two unknown men dashed toward the wagon, dragged Carter's body a short distance to a snow bank, and "tomahawked" it. They stole the victim's overcoat and the valuables in his pockets, then chased after Metcalf and his wagon. Metcalf was able to get a glimpse of them, later describing the assailants as, "one a large-sized man and the other small." A later description by the Father John Dyer in his book, *The Snow-Shoe Itinerant*, added that Metcalf said, "One of them had a broad-rimmed white hat and that both were 'men blackened'." This could have been either a description of their race or the result of the outlaws purposely darkening their faces as a disguise. This was the first description of any sort of the killers.

A second shot struck the teamster in the chest, but miraculously, it was stopped by a packet of papers in his left breast pocket. The correspondence from Denver attorney Hiram P. Bennett, which Metcalf had picked up at the Montgomery Post Office earlier in the day, saved his life. Dornick later joked in the *Rocky Mountain News Weekly* on May 16, 1863 that papers carried in a breast pocket could be called "improved patent life preservers." Metcalf's oxen spooked at a second volley, and the team took off on a run near the Cottage Grove House, whereupon the owner (Mr. Allen) came outside with his gun and scared off the attackers. Metcalf made it to Fairplay in record time, where he gave the alarm about the murder.

A posse left Fairplay and returned to the murder scene even though it was dark by then. After two hours, Carter's body was located by his brother, who was so shocked and grief-stricken that he had lingering nightmares. The body was taken into Fairplay. The distraught brother would later extract his pound of flesh in retribution.

The following morning, May 3, 1863, a large party was formed to patrol the area, with many men from Buckskin Joe volunteering to help with the hunt. Every locale within a several-mile radius was searched except the Beaver Creek area, a gulch west of Fairplay. The killers were tracked to the Platte River, where the tracks were lost in the river bed.

The brothers did not wait long for their next strike, killing again that very evening on top of Red Hill, which had been dubbed "The Bloody Red Hills" by Dornick in the *Weekly Commonwealth*, May 7, 1863. The bandits waylaid two unsuspecting travelers returning to California Gulch, located just over the Mosquito Range from Leadville. The first victim, Mr. Lehman, was returning from Central

City, where he had testified at the spring session in the U.S. District Court. Ten of his mules were stolen in Leadville on September 12, 1862, by the Leeper gang, and he appeared as the complaining witness. Lehman and his companion, a Mr. Vinton (also referred to as Segga or Seyga) were seen passing a ranch east of Red Hill around 4 p.m., and reached Red Hill one hour later.

Several hours later, a threesome from Buckskin Joe, also returning from Central City after testifying in the Leeper gang trial, discovered the bodies of Lehman and Vinton on their way home to California Gulch. An article printed in the *Weekly Commonwealth* May 7, 1863, described the victims as, "shot and tomahawked." The bodies had been robbed and stripped of clothing and their horses stolen; a personal memorandum book was taken off Lehman's person.

Soldiers from Fairplay retrieved the grisly remains and transported them back to Fairplay, where they were buried near Binkley and Shoup.

Two months later, a sojourner passing by the spot wrote to the *Daily Mining Journal* of July 23, 1864: "The shirt collar which Layman (sic) wore when killed was nailed to a Poplar sapling, and there remains to the present day."

Just as the soldiers arrived at Vinton's body on the side of the road, John Foster, walking toward Fairplay, saw the men and mistook them for the assailants. Foster ran away down Red Hill and arrived in Fairplay after dark, quite out of breath and without a coat or boots. The townsfolk thought Foster was the murderer and readied to impose the law of "Judge Lynch" upon him. Fortunately, Father Dyer recognized Foster as a godly man from California Gulch. Dyer intervened, saving Foster's neck.

Fear and trepidation rose throughout the Park. Travelers banded together, an armed contingency was formed in Buckskin Joe to find the killers, and residents were always on guard. Even some poor rabbit hunters in Mosquito Gulch were falsely reported to be the guerillas in late 1863. Dornick captured the pervasive, uneasy feeling in his letter to the *Rocky Mountain News Weekly*, May 16, 1863:

> A vague, undefined sensation of dread and fear restrains the free actions of persons who for three or four years have

been accustomed to traverse the Park and the mountains without a shadow of doubt as to their safety. None stir abroad out of sight of their respective habitations, except in parties of three or more and armed with double-barreled shotguns, double-shotted with "FFF Hazard" and No. 1 buck-shot.

Soldiers, under the command of Luther Wilson and headed by Captain John McCannon, continued scouting the county, a vast effort indeed. Marching past Pulver's ranch, located on present-day CR 90 just south of the Highway 24 turn-off, they made camp near Addleman's murder site. The following morning, on May 6, 1863, McCannon sent troops in two directions, north and east. The latter group included two soldiers, Joseph M. Lamb and William Youngh. Upon returning that evening, they reported spotting tracks on an old Indian trail.

The next day, McCannon sent the entire unit to the scene of the new tracks near Four-Mile Creek in Teller County, past the Florissant Fossil Beds. As they stole down the creek bed, they came upon an encampment with smoke still wisping into the late afternoon air. Sure that they were hot on the trail of the slayers, they temporarily back-tracked about a mile south to remain undetected.

After supper, the leader asked for volunteers for a special recognizance in the full moonlight to hunt the slayers. Seven souls signed up to walk three miles south in the cold and dark, on the lookout every moment. They bedded down until dawn then began their pursuit afresh. Lamb's later account indicated what a cold night they spent, because a fire would have signaled their location.

The group pressed ahead at first light on May 8, 1863, still traveling southward and covering many miles. The killers' tracks were now visible and soon they came to a thicket. Silently dismounting and lying in wait, it was not long before Vivian Espinosa came out to a nearby clearing where his horse was. Lamb fired. The ball hit Vivian in the chest by the ribcage. Espinosa had the wherewithal to keep a hold on his horse, pulled out a pistol, and fired at the soldiers, almost hitting the commander. Felipe Espinosa ran to see what was happening, but because Youngh was so close, the unit held their fire, allowing Felipe to scramble away. Charles Carter, whose brother had been killed at Cottage Grove, fired the second and fatal bullet at Vivian, hitting him in the head.

The group inspected the Espinosas camp site and found clothing, cooking utensils, and some of their victim's belongings, such as Harkens' glasses and horses that belonged to Lehman and Segga.

Suddenly two shots rang out from above. Felipe had made it to a rocky ledge above the clearing and was firing down upon the soldiers, who were now checking his younger brother's body. Once again Lamb executed a round, which was never returned. Felipe must have seen he was outnumbered and stole away on foot.

Exhausted and without much food, the troop set out for Cañon City, approximately thirteen miles away. They were lucky enough to find a small settlement on the way to stay overnight and some men had to be driven by wagon into town the next day due to exhaustion. The confiscated spoils were laid out for all to see, confirming these were the murderers known as the Espinosa brothers.

Dornick wrote a lengthy column about the apprehension that was published May 21, 1863, in the *Weekly Commonwealth*, including this description of how Lehman's journal had been used by one of the brothers.

> A memorandum book was found evidently taken from Mr. Lehman, in which are several pages written by the Mexican in Spanish . . . (It) states that they cannot live longer in New Mexico, and intend to kill Americans while they live; that they have killed many in South Park and are going down on the Plains to kill more. A reference to the names of "Espinosa" leaves little doubt that these Mexicans are the two brothers by the name of Espinosa that left Conejos in the winter as outlaws.

Dornick also implies that the Vivian's body had been decapitated.

Felipe eventually returned home to southern Colorado. Although he kept busy farming, the older Espinosa brother could not forget about Vivian and returned to the proverbial scene of the crime. His wanted to determine if his brother was in fact dead. After days of furtive travel, he located his brother's body in the exact place where he was killed. He cut off a portion of Vivian's foot to keep. Returning home, Felipe renewed his vow to kill Anglos, this

time recruiting a new partner—his sixteen-year-old nephew named
Jose Vincente Espinosa. The banditos rode to Sangre de Cristo Pass
close to La Veta, Colorado, where they set up a permanent camp.

Meanwhile, a military meeting was held in Conejos, Colorado,
in July 1863, including three companies of the Colorado Cavalry,
the right section of the Battery including Colonels Tappan and
Chivington, Major Whitley, Governor Evans, and John George
Nicolay, President Lincoln's Chief Secretary. Tappan had just been
appointed commander at Fort Garland on July 1, 1863. The meeting
was held at the home of Lafayette Head, the Indian Agent for the
Ute tribe. The purpose of the get-together was to hold a council
meeting between the government and the Utes to work out a treaty.

When the Espinosas got wind of the meeting, they sent a message to
the Governor Evans, demanding pardons for themselves and the return
of their family property. If their demands were not met, they threatened
to kill the governor. The *Weekly Commonwealth* of October 28, 1863, in
an article entitled "Good News from Garland," printed the threat: "'I
have now killed twenty-two Americans now, if you will give me a free
pardon of all offenses and restore my property, I will quit; otherwise
twenty-two more shall pay the penalty." Needless to say, the official did
not give in and simply increased the watch upon them via troops.

The Espinosas next preyed upon a man and woman traveling by
wagon from Trinidad to Fort Garland. Mr. Philbrook and his brother
owned a store in Trinidad; his companion was a woman named
Delores Sanchez, sometimes referred to as Lola Sanches, on her
way to visit relatives in Costilla, Colorado. Around twelve miles
from the fort, the Espinosas ambushed the couple on September 5,
1863, killing the mules and setting the wagon on fire. Philbrook
and Sanchez took off in different directions, hiding in the hillside.
Delores reportedly told Philbrook to go on without her because she
was too tired to walk all the way to Fort Garland. When another
wagon came along, she ran down to inform driver Pedro Garcia
what had happened. He suggested she get in his wagon and hide,
which she did.

In a rare showing of his face, Felipe approached, demanding
that Garcia tell him where the "Gringo" and the woman were.
Garcia admitted he had seen a man running away from the area.
At that point, Delores sat up from the wagon bed, believing that

Felipe Espinosa was a religious man and would not harm her. The killer uttered some crude remarks about her and ordered her out of the wagon. Garcia refused to release her despite Felipe's threats to kill him if he did not give the woman up. He then offered some food to the outlaws, which they accepted, and he drove off, leaving Delores to fend for herself.

The Espinosas promptly tied her up with the mule harness. She later reported that they abused her disgracefully according to Tom Tobin's memoir. When the Espinosas rode off to find Philbrook, Delores wiggled free and hid in the rocks once again. When her captors returned and saw she was gone, they rode back to their campsite. Mr. Philbrook, in the meantime, walked the twelve miles to Fort Garland, where he relayed his story.

Delores Sanchez remained hidden until morning, then started out on foot for the safety of Fort Garland. She came upon another group of travelers, but they refused to aid her out of fear for their own lives. Eight miles from the safety of the fort, she was found by a group of scouts dispatched from Fort Garland, who transported her to the welcoming outpost. Philbrook was supposedly one of the men in this scouting mission.

Colonel Tappan promptly sent a messenger out to the best frontiersman around—Thomas Tate Tobin. Hailed as their "heroic guide," Tobin agreed to the mission of hunting down and killing the Espinosas out of civic duty, unaware at the time Governor Evans had offered a handsome reward. Although Tobin initially wanted to track the killers unaided, Tappan insisted on providing some men. His adjutant, Lieutenant H. W. Baldwin plus fifteen other soldiers, including a young boy named Juan Montoya, set out at midnight on October 12, 1863. An October 28, 1863, letter to the *Weekly Commonwealth* signed by "Battery," described the adventure:

> Lt. Baldwin's party was out four days and traversed some of the ruggedest (sic) portions of the mountains to be found in these parts, yet the party with the most determined perseverance, followed the lead of their heroic guide. Perfect silence was enjoined and maintained and for three days, those men-hunters said not a word. The one absorbing idea was of the Espinosas. The thought of their name, and the hope of their

capture that burned in every breast, stilled every tongue! At night, no more fire was made than was absolutely necessary and that, so concealed, as to avoid discovery.

On October 15, 1863, Tobin picked up the trail of two people driving a team of oxen about ten miles from La Veta. He and four loyal men plus Juan Montoya snuck up close through the brush, spying a recently butchered ox and the two wanted men. As Tobin prepared to load his rifle, he stepped on a twig. The snap startled Felipe, who jumped up from where he was sitting. As he spun around, Tobin fired, hitting Felipe in the side. "Jesus favor me!" the outlaw cried. "Escape! I am killed," he shouted to Vincente. As Vincente tried to run away, Tobin yelled, "Shoot boys." They missed, but Tobin took aim and fired, striking Vincente in the back. Four of Lieutenant Baldwin's men arrived just as Felipe tried to crawl away. He sat against a tree, waving his pistol, and calling Tobin a "brute" in Spanish. Tobin asked if Felipe recognized him, but he only repeated, "Brute." (The two were distantly related through marriage.) Felipe shot at an approaching soldier but missed. Tobin's men fired again, killing the wounded man. At this point, Tobin beheaded the villain, and sent young Juan to do the same to the Espinosa nephew. With the heads in a gunnysack, the troop confiscated the outlaw's bounty and camped for the night. The next day, October 16, the group rode back to Fort Garland.

This likeness of Tom Tobin is part of a roadside sign commemorating the frontiersman located on Colorado Highway 12, south of La Veta. *Courtesy Christie Wright*

Tobin recounted the arrival in Fort Garland in an 1895 dictation:

I rode up in front of the Commanding Officer's quarters
and called for Col. Tappan. I rolled the assassins' heads out
of the sack at Col. Tappan's feet. I said, "Here Colonel, I have
accomplished what you wished. This head is Espinosa's. This
other is his companion's head and there is no mistake made."

The heads were reportedly kept in a jar at the Fort for a number
of years and later transferred to the state capitol, but they have long
since vanished.

Thus ended the "story of mad fanaticism and wanton cruelty, of
ruthless pillage and cowardly assignation, of unprovoked and cold-
blooded murder, a red page in Colorado history," as the Colorado
Springs *Gazette*, July 11, 1920, described the Espinosas brothers' saga.

However, the story did not stop there. Newspapers continued
publishing reminiscences of those involved. An especially controver-
sial account was published in 1897. John McCannon, now around
age seventy and still living in Leadville, sent a letter to the *Rocky
Mountain News*, published February 25, 1897, on the front page.
There, McCannon (erroneously referred to as McCammom) insisted
he was entitled to the $2500 reward because he—not Tobin—killed
the Espinosas. The *News* interviewed Stone, who firmly backed
Tobin as slayer of Felipe Espinosa and nephew Vincente. Whether
Tobin ever collected his full due is unknown. In 1872, the Council
of the Ninth Territorial Legislature, appropriated $500 to the famous
scout. Later, in 1895, Tobin reported that he did receive $1,500 of
the reward. But what about the remaining five hundred?

THE MURDER SITE TODAY

Red Hill Pass, where Vinton and Segga were killed, is now accessed via Highway 285; the original Red Hill Pass wagon road is now on private property. The pass is approximately eighty miles west of Denver, or three miles from the turn-off for County Road 7, at the sign for American Safari Ranch. The top of the pass is four miles north of Fairplay. Use extreme caution in this area. Many highway fatalities have occurred here.

The view from Red Hill Pass today, the site of Mora and Castillo's bloody encounter with two travelers. Red Hill is also the scene of murders by the Espinosa brothers. *Courtesy Christie Wright*

Chapter Eighteen

DARKENING the BLOODY RED HILLS
1899

One hundred fifty years ago, present-day Red Hill Pass was coined "the Bloody Red Hills," and for good reason. Two murders had been committed there in 1863 by the infamous Espinosa brothers, and on July 10, 1891, Candido Castillo and Librado Mora murdered two victims in the same area. Although Castillo and Mora had a different motive than the Espinosas, the results were the same: dead men robbed of their valuables and clothing, murdered in practically the same location.

It began on July 11, 1891, when a Mr. Smith, who worked at Webber's Livery Stable in Alma, went up the pass to look for stray stock. About one hundred yards east of the summit and fifty yards from the main road, he found the body of a middle-age, fair-complexioned man behind a log. There was a .44-caliber bullet wound under his chin; nearby was a paper bag with the name "Andy Peterson" on it.

The next day, two Fairplay men named John Fisher and Adam Reberrer discovered another body in the same vicinity. A bullet wound behind the left ear and singed hair surrounding the point of entry indicated he had been shot at close range. There was a second wound in the abdomen and another one in his arm. A letter on the man identified him as Nels O. Anderson.

The proprietor of the Fairplay House Hotel verified he had provided lunch and blankets to the two victims a few days earlier. Miner Sam Conklin, who lived near the large London Mine in Mosquito Gulch, confirmed that three Swedes had walked by his place that very afternoon and lingered awhile. They told him they had traveled on foot from Aspen to Leadville, with their final destination being Georgetown, via Fairplay. The trio was last seen in Como on the morning of July 9. No more was heard until the two bodies were discovered two days later. Many assumed that the third man, whom Conklin said seemed quieter than the other two, was the culprit because he looked "like he had done something bad, or was going to," according to the *Leadville Daily & Evening Chronicle,* July 15, 1891.

After a coroner's inquest determined that the two Swedes had in fact been murdered, the county commissioners issued a $1,000 reward and asked Governor John L. Routt to do the same. Although nearly thirty years had passed since the Espinosa murders in the Park, some still remembered those days and, given the county's remoteness, apprehension of the killers was on everyone's mind. In fact, there were several similarities to the crimes: the murders' location, the manner of death, and the fact that the victims' clothing was stolen.

One month later, Sheriff Assyria "Cy" Hall, who in addition to being sheriff was the owner of the Dolly Varden Mine on Mount Bross, received a report that two men who stopped in Buena Vista to have their horses shod were wearing some of the victims' clothing. The sheriff put a man on their trail. He traced them to Walsenburg and notified Hall to come arrest them. Apparently the suspects had boasted about their deadly escapades to two locals. The outlaws were identified as twenty-two-year-old Librado Mora and the older, more hardened, Candido Castillo.

The men had befriended each other in Huerfano County, Colorado, where both lived. In June 1891, they traveled by horse-back to Byers, Colorado, to shear sheep when the work was available, and to gamble in the evenings. The two headed south from Byers and were seen in Castle Rock and points between there and Park County the same month. Mora carried a .41 caliber silver pistol with a white handle, while Castillo had a Colt .45 that could hold either .44 or .45 cartridges.

By July 9, they were in Fairplay where they purchased more ammo at Sam Cohen's store on Front Street. Cohen was all out of .44 and .45 calibers, so Mora purchased .41 cartridges for his own gun with money furnished by his partner. After loading his gun in the store, the duo mounted up and rode off. Meanwhile, only ten miles away, Anderson and Peterson were in a store in Como. The proprietor, Mr. Pike, noticed an unusual watch that Anderson had fastened on a short, thick string and looped through a buttonhole.

Mora was arrested in Walsenburg after the sheriff took him by surprise. Officers found a .41 caliber revolver in his possession. Anderson was killed with a .41 caliber gun and Peterson with a .45. Mora was in possession of the unusual watch and was wearing a pair of pants much too large for him. While the sheriff awaited the train in Pueblo to take his prisoner to the Fairplay jail, Mora was placed in the Pueblo jail, where he removed the pants and either hid or ruined them, thereby destroying an incriminating piece of evidence. The jail guards were forced to provide him with new pants so he could continue traveling.

The next task was to go after Castillo, who had run from the lawmen. A notorious desperado, Castillo had been released from a New Mexico prison the previous summer after serving five years for killing a man in Ciboletto, New Mexico, in 1883, and killing Deputy Sheriff Juan Romero near Cabezon Station, New Mexico. Legend had it that he had done in five other men. Park County deputies Yocum and Wilson were put on his trail, and with the help of Huerfano County Deputy Sheriff Tom Brewer and area residents, they tracked him to his home in Tampa, Colorado. The lawmen watched him for two days before making their move.

When Castillo realized the lawmen had found him, he instructed his wife and friends, who were in the home, to leave. He then locked himself in a room and prepared for battle. And a battle it was, straight out of a western movie. Officers crept up and surrounded the house, shouting to Castillo to surrender, assuring him that he would be given protection.

"I will never surrender!" came his reply, firing two shots for punctuation. One bullet whizzed by so close to Brewer that he received a slight facial burn. As a diversion during the gun fight, Castillo occasionally threw items out the window, but was careful to never show his face or reveal his location in the house.

Around midnight, the bandit realized the game was up and chose to make a desperate break for liberty. Throwing open the front door, he dashed out, six shooters blazing in each hand.

Librado Mora was sentenced to death upon being convicted of first degree murder, but his sentence was later commuted. *Courtesy Colorado State Archives*

Miraculously, he did not hit anyone in spite of being well known as a crack shot. Officers promptly returned fire, and one of their many bullets hit Castillo. He fell into the brush and yelled, "Come on, you have got me." Only after one of Castillo's friends at the scene confiscated his gun did the officers feel safe in approaching.

Castillo surrendered, and was carried to his house, where the group saw that he had been shot in the thigh. The men carefully washed and dressed the wound, and for a while, it seemed that he would survive, but he died several hours later. Castillo was able to give a final statement as to Mora's involvement, verifying that the younger man was actually an unwilling participant in the murderous events.

Librado Mora's trial was held at the end November 1891, after he had spent several months in jail. He was defended by Walsenburg attorney R. A. Quillan, who argued that the case was based on circumstantial evidence. The prisoner was said to be well-educated and reportedly took a great interest in the legal doings. On December 3, the jury found him guilty of first-degree murder. Not one jury member had a Hispanic surname. This was the second Park County killing requiring the ultimate punishment; Sims preceded him eleven years earlier and two more would come after Mora. As Judge Samuel P. Dale read the death sentence, Mora maintained his composure.

Sheriff Hall and Deputy Wilson whisked Mora away to Cañon City, where he was scheduled to be hung during Christmas week; however, his execution was continued until the second week of January. Mora was spared in January after his attorney applied to the Colorado Supreme Court for a "writ of error," which stayed the execution until the court could review the case. They concluded this task at the end of November 1893. The judgment was affirmed the week of Christmas, and execution was scheduled for the first week of January 1894. Once again, Mora was spared, this time by his own sentencing judge, the Honorable Samuel P. Dale, who wrote to the State Board of Pardons recommending a commutation of sentence based on Mora's youth and the fact that he was induced into crime by his cohort, a "desperate ruffian." The governor granted a thirty-day reprieve, and Mora's friends and relatives submitted a petition on his behalf.

On February 3, 1894, the Board of Pardons recommended executive clemency, commuting the sentence to life in prison. Colorado State Senator Casimiro Barela, from Trinidad, was instrumental in securing his commutation. The *Fairplay Flume* blasted the decision, calling Governor Waite's administration "a travesty."

Mora submitted a pardon request based on his assertion that he did not actually commit murder but only helped rob the bodies. It was very possible that Castillo used Mora's gun to shoot Anderson, and furthermore, Castillo had absolved Mora of any wrongdoing on his deathbed. This request was either denied or delayed, because in March 1898, he pleaded for a pardon a second time. The decision did not go his way. The Board concluded it "was not convinced that it would be a wise move to give Moro his liberty."

Mora must have been released shortly after 1902 because by 1910, he was living in the little town of Pryor, north of Trinidad. Two children with his name are listed in the 1910 U. S. Census, the oldest one was age ten. His wife's name was Felipa. The family later moved to Walsenburg. By 1920, Mora had died.

THE MURDER SITE TODAY

Red Hill Pass is now accessed via Highway 285; the original Red Hill Pass wagon road is now on private property. The pass is approximately eighty miles west of Denver, or three miles from the turn-off for County Road 7, at the sign for American Safari Ranch. The top of the pass is four miles north of Fairplay. Many highway fatalities have occurred here, so use extreme caution in this area.

The Central Towns

Get ready for one wild ride through the central towns of Como, Fairplay, and Alma. Fairplay and Alma sprang up around the hard metal mining industry, while Como, twelve miles north of Fairplay, developed as a railroad supply center and a coal mining hub.

The very first Park County towns of Hamilton, Tarryall, and Buckskin Joe are now extinct as are many the smaller settlements, such as Dudley, Quartzville, and Timberline.

COMO

Como was a railroad and coal mining town, formed as a supply center for the Denver South Park & Pacific railroad as it worked its way up from Platte Canyon into South Park in 1879. A roundhouse, hotel, and depot were the main anchor buildings. Workers were housed in tents, and Como was called the "Tented Town:" Sixty to seventy-five tents were set up at the end of the line. The tents served as business sites and workers' quarters. It is said Como was created in thirty days.

Houses for the workers and their families soon replaced tents. Como was considered a company town, although the workers were expected to construct their own homes. With plenty of carpenters in town, this done fairly was easily.

The average freight was twenty cars daily—five hauled general merchandise, five were loaded with hay, and the remainder brought in machinery and coke. The outgoing train was loaded with ten cars full of ore and bullion.

The railroad owned the coal seam in Como and when first discovered, the vein was between six- and eight-feet wide. It was estimated that by the winter of 1879, 300 tons per day were mined.

The railroad began laying people off in 1910, causing the town's population to dwindle quickly. Once the train stopped running in 1937, Como nearly became a ghost town but today it once again has year-round inhabitants.

FAIRPLAY

Fairplay was designated the county seat in 1867 after the Buckskin Joe mines west of present-day Alma played out and the population there greatly decreased. The name Fairplay, or Fair Play, once called South Park City, is interesting and several differing legends describe how the name came to be. The most common story is that when the rich gold was discovered in Hamilton in 1859, a "rush" soon followed. Miners swarmed in and staked numerous claims, driving the price sky-high for the late-comers. Frustrated, some begrudgingly coined the area "Grab-All," and settled further on down the Platte River where they began prospecting. By dubbing the new diggings "Fair Play," they made a statement that countered the greedy practices in Hamilton. The town's main business district burned to the ground in 1873 but was soon rebuilt.

Both the Park County Sheriff and Deputy Sheriff were headquartered in Fairplay; this may or may not have kept a lid on the in-town crime rate and the town killings were sensational. Some local shootings, although not fatal, involved town marshals.

ALMA

The town of Alma developed when the Boston and Colorado Smelting Company erected a smelter there in 1872 to process the rich silver ores from the newly discovered silver mines on the nearby Mounts Lincoln and Bross. These included the Russia and Moose Mines. As with Fairplay's name, there are several different stories as to how the camp was named but the popular one is that Alma was the name of a prominent citizen's wife, a Mrs. Janes. This could well have been Addison M. Janes, deputy postmaster, who briefly named a settlement for himself near Alma called "Janesville."

With this silver boom, the precursor to the famous Leadville excitement, Alma became a hub of mining activity and support services quickly sprang up in town—general stores, mining supply outfits and, of course, the ever-present saloons. Saloons served as a vital gathering point for the many newcomers to the camps and provided a focal point for socializing along with the drinking. The population influx was not without its problems, as we will see below.

The following stories often showcase the sensational journalism style of crime reporting in the late 1800's. The images created by these writers are still quite vivid 130 years later, especially when visiting the old courthouse in Fairplay. And about that window. . . .

Many of the original murder sites are difficult to pinpoint because the buildings are long since gone or information recorded while they were standing was not specific. Some were "flash in the pan" businesses with minimal documentation about their location. Other buildings stand today as a silent reminder of Park County's exciting past.

Pat Golden's shed was located across from the Pacific Hotel, shown in this turn of the century photo. The hotel burned down on November, 9, 1896, and the Como Eating House was built on the site. The structure is now a restaurant and B&B. *Courtesy Park County Local History Archives # 914. Source: Park County Historical Society*

Chapter Nineteen

DOOLITTLE'S DASTARDLY DEED
1880

Pat Golden, one of the railroad section bosses, owned a frame house near the railroad track west of the Como railroad station. Directly behind his house sat an old, nondescript shed valued at all of two dollars. Another resident, William Clark, claimed he was the shed's owner, having purchased it from the old-timer who had built it. Golden and Clark already had an established rivalry over another matter involving a "board bill," and things weren't easy between the two.

On October 7, 1880, Clark hired ranch hand John Doolittle to dismantle the shed and cart it away. Doolittle, age twenty-six, had relocated to Colorado from Iowa two years earlier. According to a Denver newspaper account, he was said to be a very quiet man and not given to drinking. He lived in Como but worked at George Lechner's ranch just north of town. Lechner was a well-known "pioneer of the Park," who discovered coal on his land in the 1860s. Little did Lechner know that twenty-two years later, he himself would be sitting in the Park County courtroom listening to another trial involving a Como shooting: his own son's murder trial. But that's another story.

On that crisp autumn morning, Clark and Doolittle drove up in Clark's wagon and immediately began taking down the shed. Hearing a noise outside his house, Golden came out to see what was going on. He immediately ordered the two to leave the shed alone, explaining that the little building was on railroad property. Golden's brother soon entered the fray, trying to knock Doolittle off a box he was standing on to deter him from the destruction.

Stepping down, Doolittle calmly pulled a revolver out of his bootleg and shot Golden near the heart.

Golden staggered to his house with the assistance of stunned friends while Doolittle went back to his nearby cabin and grabbed his rifle. He passed Arthur O'Neil, the saloonkeeper at the Elkhorn Saloon, who noticed the rifle and jokingly asked Doolittle why he was going hunting so early in the season. The shooter explained what had happened and agreed to surrender himself upon O'Neil's advice. They hopped in Doolittle's wagon and drove back to Elkhorn's.

Doolittle was lucky that he chanced to meet O'Neil. The railroad men had armed themselves, preparing to take Doolittle at gunpoint and make him "swing." Some of the more level-headed men insisted O'Neil transport the murderer to Fairplay and into the hands of Sheriff Ifinger, which he did. Golden subsequently died from his injuries, and Ifinger took his new charge to Denver for safekeeping once the word got out that Golden had died.

By the next month, John Doolittle was back in the Park County jail and described in the *Fairplay Flume* of November 25, 1880, as "almost prostrated from fear or anguish over the result of his hasty act." It is not known if this is because he was sorry he was caught or remorseful over killing a man. Doolittle remained in jail until his trial by Judge Joseph Helm, a stern-looking jurist who was elected to the Colorado Supreme Court two years later.

At midnight on April 28, 1881, the jury returned a verdict of manslaughter after deliberating only a few hours. As was standard practice at the time, a motion for a new trial was filed. It was denied, and the defendant was sentenced to five years' hard labor in the penitentiary. The sheriff whisked Doolittle away to Cañon City the following day.

Three years later, a "generous" Governor James B. Grant pardoned the inmate based on a petition signed by the trial judge, then District Attorney Webster Ballinger, and some jury members and friends, extolling young Doolittle's previously good character and claiming the shooting was in self-defense, although at the time of the crime, the *Flume* described it as a "cold-blooded and unprovoked killing" in its October 7, 1880 edition.

Doolittle apparently returned to the scene of the crime. He was living in Park County in 1885, according to the state census of that year. In 1892, he sold a lot in Como to another party. Genealogy records show that in 1920, when he was 68, he was living in Arizona. Presumably he stayed out of trouble.

THE SHOOTING SITE TODAY

The shed where Doolittle shot Patrick Golden was located just west of the Como depot. The depot is currently undergoing renovations and is on private property but can easily be viewed from the road.

John Doolittle was 28 when his mug shot was taken in May 1881. *Courtesy Colorado State Archives*

Montag's Saloon today. Gallagher waited for his victim near the saloon. The diagonal corner entrance was added in the 1930s and was not part of the original structure. *Courtesy Sean Brubaker, Evoke Images*

Chapter Twenty

FISHING for TROUBLE
1882

Railroad work is hard work, and some of the men who came into the county to work the rails were hard workers, hard drinkers, and hard-headed. James Gallagher, age thirty, was one such individual. The five-foot-four Irishman was a section hand in Como. Another hard-drinking hand was Martin O'Gorman, who was older than Gallagher.

On April 29, 1882, the two were told to shovel some of the debris on the track near the Como roundhouse. Full of liquor as usual, Gallagher pushed his coworker so hard that they both fell to the ground. O'Gorman got up, dusted himself off, and walked away from the quarrel.

This was only a prequel to a much worse altercation that happened the next day. It was Sunday afternoon, and a crowd had gathered at the Elkhorn Saloon. O'Gorman was at the bar as usual, drinking with another buddy. Gallagher seated himself next to the stove near the coal box.

Seeing his rival, O'Gorman got off his bar stool, walked behind Gallagher, and picked up a hatchet that was used to break up coal. With the flat side of the weapon, he smacked Gallagher hard across the side of his face and head. Gallagher jumped up and tried to get at his attacker, but the other patrons held him back. Disgusted, Gallagher walked out of the saloon, vowing vengeance. He proceeded to Justice W. B. Fowler's residence to swear out a warrant. Fowler had received his appointment only four weeks earlier, but was a well-known and respected citizen of the area.

A fishplate is a foot-long piece of rail, shown here with four bolts, that attaches two separate rails together. *Courtesy Becky Young, Becky Young Photography*

Gallagher got his wound dressed with a large bandage wrapped around his head, which made him look much like a mummy. This must have been a sight as he plodded back down to the railroad tracks and picked up a discarded fishplate, a heavy iron bar that connects two rails together. Back in Como's business district, he sat down on the sidewalk near Montag's Saloon, with the large hunk of iron hidden behind beer kegs.

Suddenly, O'Gorman burst out of the Elkhorn's swinging wood doors, so drunk he could hardly walk. Staggering toward Gallagher, he collapsed in a stupor. He tried to get up, but Gallagher ordered, "Lie down until the marshal comes." A sixth sense must have warned the inebriated fellow to protect himself, because he slowly began filling his pockets full of stones. After a time, O'Gorman was able to roust himself up and wander off, whereupon Gallagher stood up, grabbed his weapon, and concealed it in his vest.

Gallagher started after him with one thing in mind: revenge. O'Gorman did not get far before the Gallagher felled him a fierce blow to the back of his head, knocking him to the ground. He then struck him two more times on the head, tossed the fishplate, and took off on a run. He was apprehended minutes later by Deputy Sheriff Metz and taken to jail by the Town Constable Mullen.

O'Gorman was carried to Flynn's Boarding House, where he was cared for. Dr. Marris arrived a few hours later, pronouncing the injury a serious skull fracture with no hope of recovery. The railroad hand died the following morning without ever regaining his senses.

Another doctor, Dr. Lameter, came the next day to hold the coroner's inquest. After hearing the testimony of many eyewitnesses, the six-man panel decided an autopsy was in order. A five-inch portion of O'Gorman's cracked skull was saved as evidence for trial.

Gallagher was later taken to Denver for both safekeeping and to deter him from a third escape attempt from the Fairplay jail. His first attempt was on July 4, 1882. He had been ordered him to empty the slop bucket at Kennedy's Restaurant, but, responding to freedom's call, he bolted into the night and headed for the forest, where he almost made good his escape. The sheriff fired two warning shots in the air, which alerted nearby residents, who soon were in hot

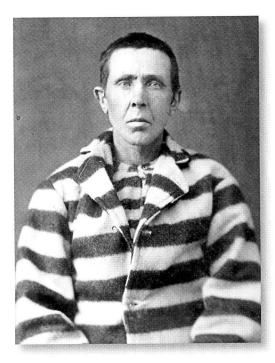

Inmate # 783, James Gallagher, wears the standard prison uniform issued to him in 1882. *Courtesy Colorado State Archives.*

pursuit of the scoundrel. Another man on horseback managed to head him off, and Gallagher was returned to his confines. No details of his second escape attempt are known.

James Gallagher was convicted of second-degree murder in early September 1882, whereupon Judge Joseph Helm sentenced him to hard labor in prison for his natural life. No premeditation was found. When asked his feelings about his sentence by a *Flume* reporter, he replied quietly, "Oh, that's all right."

As was the legal custom of the time, when the inmate applied for a pardon twelve years later, the trial judge himself recommended Gallagher be set free. So did then State Senator Pease, who "talked so well that the board thought that Gallagher had been punished enough." Another reason is that the law for "life in prison" changed from a fixed life term to from ten years to life at the court's discretion. Gallagher was a free man after earning the dubious distinction of being the oldest inmate in the Colorado prison system. He was fifty-one. Compare that to the Colorado Department of Corrections 2011 statistics, where nearly 2,500 inmates are in their fifties.

THE MURDER SITE TODAY

Montag's Saloon still stands, empty and dilapidated. The original owner, George Montag, was a rancher and miner. His saloon was shut down in 1916, shortly before Prohibition took effect. An unusual building, it sports a diagonal corner piece added in the 1930s. It stands south of the Como Depot.

Family photo of victim Augustus Cornog, killed by John Laughlin, who was acquitted of the crime. *Courtesy Robert A. Cornog*

Chapter Twenty-One

A KILLING OVER KEROSENE
1879

I n the fall of 1879, Como had a labor dispute coined "The Como War" by the local newspaper. It pitted Chinese coal miners against the Italians. Como's coal beds, discovered in the mid-1860s on several area ranches, were among the smaller coal fields in the state. The largest coal mine was called the King Mine, after County Clerk A. J. King. It included six smaller mines with various levels.

Italian immigrant miners moved into the area to work, naming the nearby little town after the beautiful village of Como, Italy. The going wage of $2.50 a day was considered generous for the times.

Soon the Denver, South Park & Pacific Railroad brought Chinese workers to work the lower shaft of the King Mine at their bargain rate. The Italians began to worry that they would lose their jobs to the "Celestials," as they called the Chinese. Their fears were realized in November 1879 when two Italian workers were replaced by Chinese laborers. Language barriers, dangerous working conditions, and long workdays contributed to tensions between the two groups as well.

The Italian miners asked the working boss, E. L. Thayer, to stop employing the Chinese, but he claimed he would have to talk to the company first. A confrontation quickly ensued, with differing accounts of what happened. One version claimed that Thayer was beaten and someone put a gun put to his head and fired, but that the bullet only grazed his scalp. Another version was that Thayer waved his gun around and one of the miners stepped up and hit him in the mouth. Either way, Thayer ended up leaving, and the

Italians proceeded to the Chinese workers' shanties and ordered them to leave, which they did.

Governor Evans stepped in, siding with the railroad company's plan to hire Chinese workers. In a Thanksgiving Day letter to the *Rocky Mountain News*, he called the Italian miners' wages "extravagant." Evans ordered twenty armed guards from the Rocky Mountain Detective Association to Como to protect the Chinese, and he dismissed the Italians on the grounds they could not mine the coal quickly enough, causing loaded railroad cars to sit idle in the freight yards. Their dismissal was dramatic—as they reported to the King early one morning to go to work, the guards were lined up, preventing them from entering the mine.

One of these guards was Augustus "Gus" Cornog (also referred to as Cornig or Conrad). He was described as a tall, muscular man with a huge, tawny moustache, by the *Rocky Mountain News* of December 11, 1879. Another guard was John W. Laughlin (spelled McLaughlin in some newspapers). The two were assigned to guard the lower portion of the mine under the direction of Denver Deputy Sheriff W. A. Smith. The twenty armed guards were housed in cabins in Como, with Cornog and Laughlin bunking in with two other guards.

On December 9, 1879, Laughlin had plans to take the train back to Denver but missed his train. He returned to the cabin, where he had supper with his fellow guards. While they were sitting around the fire after supper, Cornog came in the cabin with some coal oil and threw it on the flames to get it going. Some of the coal oil splashed on Laughlin's pants, and on December 13, 1879, Laughlin told a *Rocky Mountain News* reporter that this conversation ensued:

"Cornog, I don't want my clothes covered with oil. I can't afford to buy a new suit very soon," protested Laughlin.

"What have you got to say about it?" retorted the big man.

"You are always trying to aggravate someone," protested Laughlin.

"God damn you, I'll shoot you," snarled Cornog, at the same time drawing his revolver. With a fire poker he held in the other hand, Cornog whacked Laughlin on the arm. Another guard named Bill Mason intervened and began guiding Laughlin toward the door, saying, "This is pretty rough, but I guess you had better take it all in and have no quarrel."

"I don't want to have any fuss," asserted Laughlin, looking around.

Suddenly, he saw Cornog pointing a revolver at both of them. Mason stepped aside to get out of range, admonishing, "Cornog, you had better put that down or I'll take a hand in this." Cornog then took his revolver down.

In the meantime, Laughlin had taken a rifle from where it hung on the wall. (Rifles were the standard issue weapons to the mine guards).

"I think it is mean of you to draw a revolver on a man when he is not armed," said Laughlin.

Cornog then made a movement as though he was about to raise his revolver, and Laughlin answered with firepower. Just as he pulled the trigger, someone opened the door, causing the light to blow out.

"Will someone light the lamp?" shouted Laughlin, to which a guard named McFadden complied. Laughlin wanted to see where he had hit the big fellow. The bullet had struck the victim in the head and exited his neck, killing him instantly.

"This is pretty bad," said Mason, looking at Cornog on the floor.

"I know it," replied the shooter quietly. Mason went off to find Deputy Smith to report the incident.

Laughlin maintained his cool and, instead of running away, walked up to the engine house at the coal mine. There he sat, rifle across his lap, until Smith approached and he willingly surrendered. Later, Smith announced that Laughlin had already been fired because he was quarrelsome.

A coffin arrived from Denver from Brown's undertaking establishment, but Cornog's size and build required his remains be placed in the shipping box that had held the casket. His brother, Isaac, from Philadelphia, requested the body be sent to Denver, where it would then be forwarded to Pennsylvania for burial.

Word soon got out that Cornog was to have been married— some said on the very day of his death—to a lady from New Orleans named Miss Lee. In Gus Cornog's possessions was a letter from Miss Lee Heber to Gus's brother dated February 24, 1879. Her heart-wrenching correspondence leaves us wondering what transpired between the two as she speaks of being cruelly wronged, her life of misery, and a new burden on her hands. She also mentions a "blood-curdling" incident she dared not talk about.

Word also spread that Laughlin had shot Cornog in self-defense and that the courts and citizens alike would go easy on him. Apparently he didn't have to worry about his neck being "stretched," unlike his jail cohorts Cicero C. Sims and John J. Hoover, but he was transported to the Denver jail for safekeeping just the same. "I am confident I can obtain enough witnesses to prove that I acted in self-defense and I am perfectly confident about my case," Laughlin told a *Rocky Mountain News* reporter on December 14, 1879.

Laughlin was returned to the Fairplay jail pending his court trial before Judge Thomas M. Bowen in the spring of 1880. The two trials ahead of his were those of John J. Hoover and Cicero C. Sims (See chapters 25 and 28). Hoover was lynched the night before Laughlin's trial, and Sims received an execution sentence. When it was Laughlin's turn on the docket, his trial was continued until November 1880. This was because the excitement of Hoover's lynching and vigilante threats at Sims's trial ran the good judge and his wife out of town the afternoon of Laughlin's scheduled trial, leaving Laughlin high and dry. Laughlin was on the receiving end of what came to be called "the court that never adjourned," but it literally saved his neck.

This meant another half year in the Denver jail, a price the suspect was willing to pay to let things settle down a bit in Park County.

The trial finally came off on November 10, 1880, in front of Judge Thomas A. McMorris, who was appointed to succeed Judge Bowen, who had suddenly retired after the Fairplay fiasco. According to the *Fairplay Flume* on November 11, 1880:

> The evidence showed that J.W. Laughlin, who was held for the murder, committed the deed at a time when he considered his own life in danger and the provocation offered by Cornog, together with other extenuating circumstances, led the jury to give the verdict of not guilty and after a year of confinement awaiting his trial, Laughlin walked forth a free man.

Why Hoover was lynched but Laughlin went free is a mystery to this day. He perhaps owed his life to Mrs. Thomas M. Bowen, who insisted her husband leave Fairplay immediately without conducting Laughlin's trial. If that had been the case, Laughlin stood a good chance of either a lengthy prison sentence or a death sentence, given the community's frustration with Hoover and Sims.

In the years following his acquittal, Laughlin moved back to his home state of Ohio and married Rachael Gordon on March 1, 1882. They had several children. Laughlin died at the age of seventy-two in Miami, Florida, in 1929.

THE MURDER SITE TODAY

The exact location of the Como cabin where the mine guards lived is unknown, but many buildings from the period can be seen Como today. Como is an enjoyable town to visit.

The Como Odd Fellows Hall in 2008. *Courtesy Christie Wright.*

Chapter Twenty-Two

MURDER at the CHRISTMAS DANCE
1902

One week before Christmas in 1902, a minstrel show was held in the Como Odd Fellows Hall for the tight-knit community of railroad workers and engineers, who enjoyed getting together for various occasions. The show was followed with a dance. Well-known resident Richard "Dick" Lechner, whose father was George Lechner, a "pioneer of the Park," had recently sold his saloon business. The sale of his saloon did little to slow down Dick's alcohol consumption. He continued to tend bar for friends, most recently working at Montag's Saloon. He managed to keep his good reputation intact until the early morning of December 18, 1902.

The night before at the Christmas party, Lechner danced with a young lady. The couple turned to sit down, but all the seats were taken. Lechner asked William Hayden, who was known locally as "Billy the Kid," to get up and give the lady his seat. Hayden refused. Words were exchanged, and Hayden stormed off to the other side of the room.

In a few minutes, a young boy came up to Lechner, informing him that Mr. Hayden now wished to speak with him. Thinking that the matter would soon be settled, Lechner approached and Hayden extended his right hand as if to shake hands. Instead, Hayden struck Lechner a blow with his left arm, knocking him down, and began pummeling him. Onlookers quickly separated the two but were unable to separate Lechner from his desire to retaliate.

Lechner left the danceand went to his boarding room where he retrieved a Winchester rifle. Close to 1:30 a.m., he started back toward the dance hall when he spied Hayden coming out of a building about twenty-five feet in front of him. Hayden turned partially around, pointed his finger at Lechner, and called him an obscene name. With that, Lechner let Billy the Kid have it.

The first shot threw the victim backward. The shooter pressed on, firing three more times at the wounded man on the ground. According to the December 26, 1902, *Fairplay Flume*, "One shot broke Hayden's leg near the hip, two missed and the last shot entered the back part of the head, passing entirely through and coming out near the outer angle of the right eye." A gruesome sight indeed for the partygoers at Christmastime. One newspaper reported that Lechner did not try to run away and that he remained at the scene until Sheriff Polluck arrived from Fairplay.

A coroner's inquest panel was convened later that day and determined Lechner fired with "felonious intent," meaning he could be jailed and charged with murder. The sheriff duly took him to Fairplay and jailed him. The inmate appeared before Justice of the Peace C. S. Wells the following day. Wells set the preliminary examination for December 30, 1902, which meant that Lechner would spend Christmas in jail. George Lechner came from Denver, where he had lived for many years, to attend his son's trial, and it was rumored he would hire an expensive Denver attorney to defend his son. None other than former Colorado State Speaker of the House Edwin M. Hurlbut was retained. Hurlbut was also the former district attorney for the First Judicial District and had served as Creede's first mayor.

Billy Hayden's mother, Sarah, traveled from Como to Fairplay to hear testimony from Lechner as to what happened. On the way, she broke her right arm when her horse team ran out of control and tipped the buggy.

Twenty-two witnesses were called at the preliminary hearing, only eight of those testified for the defense. Testimony and rebuttal continued well into the night of January 2, 1903. The defense presented two arguments: first, that Lechner thought Hayden had a gun in his hand when he came out of the hall and pointed at Lechner; and second, that Lechner was drunk at the time and did not realize what he was doing. The other main focus was bail, which was "argued at length and citations read from similar cases and Supreme Court rulings." Justice Wells, however, refused bail and bound Lechner over to the next term of the District Court, four months hence.

District Court Judge Morton S. Bailey presided that spring, granting a special trial session on June 22, 1903, so that Lechner's new attorney, Henry M. Teller, could prepare a defense of his good friend's son. The father of the defendant and the mother of the victim were also in court. Both in their eighties, it must have been a sad day for these Como old-timers. Most of the Como townsfolk came as well, many feeling sorry for George Lechner, with his snow-white head bowed most of the time. Arguments on both sides took up two and one-half hours, and the case was given to the jury at 6 p.m. on Monday night, June 22.

Two days of wrangling did not bring a unanimous verdict, and the jurors were discharged on Thursday, June 25, at 5 p.m. Five jurors voted for manslaughter and five for acquittal. Lechner testified in his own behalf, stating that at the time he thought Hayden had a gun but now he was not so sure.

Because of the hung jury, Lechner was bound over to the next court term but was released on $5,000 bail. October 22, 1903, saw another jury convened only to end in the same way—this time, five for acquittal and seven for conviction. This scenario repeated itself yet again at the 1904 spring term of court, and it must have seemed to all that a verdict would never be reached. Indeed, it was continued again to October 1904 by agreement of both parties.

There are no newspaper accounts of the trial specifically or the final verdict. While the outcome is unknown, we do know that Dick Lechner married the girl from the dance, Marcia Moore, in Cripple Creek on January 18, 1905, which "lends an element of romance to the case," as the *Flume* sang the week following the wedding.

THE MURDER SITE TODAY

The original Odd Fellows Hall still stands but is now a private residence. It is located near the Como Depot and the Como Eating House. The Odd Fellows Hall is easily identified by the unusual octagon-shaped addition added in the 1960s,

The grave marker in Como Cemetery where Anna and Sam Speas buried three infants. *Courtesy Sean Brubaker, Evoke Images*

Chapter Twenty-Three

COBBLER KILLS MARSHAL COOK
1896

On Friday, April 6, 1896, around 10:30 p.m., Como Town Marshal A. E. Cook went to investigate a noisy gathering at the two-room house of Levi J. Streeter, the local cobbler. Streeter's combined house and shop was near the corner of Eighth and Broadway Streets, directly across from the post office. Delaney's saloon was three doors down, and Montag's Saloon was two doors up, across the street.

Cook, who had lived in the Como area for a number of years, had recently been reelected marshal for a second two-year term. He was well known and well liked, and as the former foreman in the Como railroad shop, he had many friends among the "railroaders." About forty-five years of age, he was the head of a family with three young daughters. Streeter had lived in Como several years as well, and the two were acquainted.

As the marshal approached Streeter's front door, the house was dark save for the light of a lamp coming from the back room. Cook knocked. Streeter was armed when he threw the door open. The two immediately began arguing. Streeter yelled, "You son-of-a-bitch, if you come in my house, I'll kill you!" He fired once, hitting Cook dead-on in the chest. The marshal fell where he stood, facedown inside the front door with the toes of his boots resting on the door sill. Streeter then pounded the lawman's head with the gun butt, crushing his skull. Finally, he finished his victim off with two more bullets to the head.

Immediately after the shots were fired, a commotion came from the rear of the home, followed by the sound of breaking glass. Two women bailed out the back window, and at least one of them was cut in the process. Two unknown men ran out Streeter's front door, requiring them to step over Cook's dead form in the doorway.

Streeter stepped out onto the sidewalk and walked toward two of the witnesses, James Delaney and Charles Montag, the saloon owners. The two had stepped outside to investigate the disturbance, along with Edwin Montag, Charles's brother. According to testimony by witnesses at the coroner's inquest hearing, the following conversation took place:

"Come, get out of the way or we may get shot ourselves," said Delaney as Streeter approached.

In a moment, Streeter reached them with the gun tucked under his arm and spoke: "I've killed a man in here."

"Who is it?" Delaney asked, eyeing the large weapon.

"I don't know," Streeter replied. "He (the man) came to the door and says, 'I want all the money you got,' and I shot him." Streeter didn't mention the brief argument at his front door or his vicious gun-butt attack on the victim.

It was Edwin Montag who took a look over the threshold and announced, "It is Cook."

Streeter was subsequently arrested by Deputy Sheriff James Link and Constable Lyons, who immediately took him to the Fairplay jail for safekeeping. During questioning, Streeter claimed that when he answered the door, a man ordered him to put his hands up. Assuming he was going to be held up, he shot what he thought was an unknown robber. Rumor had it that Streeter dealt in considerable amounts of gold and silver, and had money in his cabin. Rumor also had it that Streeter thought the man who knocked on his door might have been engineer Sam Speas looking for his wife, Anna. Speas—a big man at six feet tall, two hundred pounds, and strong to boot—had previously warned the cobbler to stay away from his wife. Streeter may have had good reason to fear the engineer.

Anna Blythe had married Sam Speas in Boulder, Colorado, in 1886 when she was seventeen; Sam was eleven years her senior. Described as a beautiful young woman, she was quite popular in Boulder, where her family had moved from Humboldt, Kansas. The newlyweds moved to Como in 1887 after Sam was hired as engineer there. Engineers were held in the highest regard, and young Anna may have been the envy of other women.

Although the couple wanted to start a family, Anna lost three babies between 1887 and 1894; they are buried under one marker in the Como cemetery. Her sister Nellie in Boulder had the same difficulty. Upset over her painful loss, the bereft mother began drinking, possibly the reason she was at Streeter's on the night of the murder. Her friend, Mrs. Lillian Kennedy Robinson, was also at Streeter's that night. Her husband divorced her soon after the scandal broke.

The newspapers immediately picked up on the fact that married women were cavorting with men, and had a field day with it. The *Flume* on April 12, 1894, described the group: "[A] little party of men and women of doubtful character to say the least, were holding a jollification in Streeter's place, finally becoming quite convivial and noisy through partaking of frequent draughts of beer."

Witness A. J. Cushman, a teacher in Como, reported that he was just about asleep when shots were fired. Afterward, he heard some women talking and watched out his bedroom window as they hurried up to a corner of the street. One of the ladies was sobbing, leading him to conclude that someone was hurt.

During a preliminary hearing, Mrs. Speas and Mrs. Robinson were questioned but denied knowing anything about what went on at the front of the house. It was true they did not see the actual shooting, and they claimed they did not hear a thing.

Mrs. Cook, the distraught widow, prevailed upon the sheriff to arrest the women as accessories, which he did. Mrs. Robinson and Mrs. Speas were escorted to Fairplay on Saturday, April 14, remaining there until Monday, when they posted bond. In the unlikely event there were no male inmates in the county jail that weekend, the women would have presumably been incarcerated there; otherwise, it is possible they were held at the hospital.

Streeter also had a preliminary hearing, but the case was given to a grand jury. He was therefore remanded to custody without bond for a month until the jury was convened. On May 16, the trio appeared in front of a justice of the peace, and Streeter was bound over for trial. He was represented by Judge Webster Ballinger. Four days later, four friends of Cook's hired prominent Fairplay attorney Charles A. Wilkin to help Vinton G. Holliday prosecute the case.

The coroner's inquest panel took eight hours to make its final determination:

> We the jury after careful examination of witnesses and due deliberation affirm that deceased came to his death as the result of gun shot wounds caused by bullets fired from a gun held in the hands of L.J. Streeter and therefore recommend that he be bound over to appear before the District Court. Whether or not feloniously we do not feel justified in saying.

Streeter's trial began on the last day of May 1894. The prosecution was represented by District Attorney Holliday, assisted by Wilkin. Streeter's attorneys were Ballinger and Judge George Pease. The jury deliberated until 1 a.m. on June 2, but reached no verdict. Finally, after being allowed a few hours' sleep, the jury reached a unanimous decision at 8:30 a.m. Word spread of the pending verdict, and a crowd packed the courtroom that Saturday morning. Levi J. Streeter was found "guilty as charged in the indictment" of first-degree murder.

Speas and Robinson were found not guilty of accessory to murder. Robinson was the only defendant who testified in her own behalf; defense counsel did not call Streeter or Speas to the stand. A motion for a new trial was requested and denied. Streeter was sentenced to execution the week of June 24, 1894, and was taken to Cañon City.

A ninety-day respite was granted during the week his execution had been scheduled, and his attorney filed for another continuance to prepare the appeal, which was granted on July 6. A third continuance, this one for sixty days, was later issued, beginning on December 30, so he could "perfect his appeal" to the Colorado Supreme Court.

Streeter also filed for a pardon, resulting in a flood of letters from his friends to the governor's office on February 1, 1896. The *Rocky Mountain News* reported on that date: "The letter which Streeter sends to the Board of Pardons is illegible, but the writer claims self-defense as his reason for killing the marshal."

That month, in a surprise move, the Board of Pardons recommended commuting the sentence from death to life imprisonment at hard labor for the following reasons: 1) the question remained whether the jury deliberated a sufficient amount of time to reach the verdict, given that they'd only had a few hours of sleep; 2) the "peculiar circumstances under which the crime was committed"; 3) the commutation recommendations submitted by the trial judge, district attorney, and numerous Como citizens.

After all the appeals, Streeter died in prison from consumption, only two months after receiving the commuted sentence, on April 9, 1896. According to prison records, he is not buried in "Woodpecker Hill," the portion of Cañon City's Greenwood Pioneer Cemetery reserved for inmates. Presumably family members retrieved the body and buried Levi J. Streeter elsewhere.

THE SHOOTING SITE TODAY

Marshal Cook was buried in Denver. His name was added to the National Law Enforcement Officer's Memorial Wall in Washington D.C., in May 2010.

Levi Streeter, sentenced to be executed for the murder of Como Town Marshal A.E. Cook, is shown here in his prison mug shot in June 1894. Streeter had served less than two years when he died in prison in Cañon City from tuberculosis. *Courtesy Colorado State Archives.*

The streets of Fairplay as they looked during the 1880s when the Red Light Dance Hall was thriving. The dance hall building was destroyed by fire in 1883. *Courtesy Park County Local History Archives # 3292. Source: Ed and Nancy Bathke Collection*

Chapter Twenty-Four

THE RED LIGHT DANCE HALL CURSE
1879

T rue to its name, the Red Light Dance Hall in Fairplay was a
hotbed of illicit activity. At least one Alma citizen "betook"
herself to the Red Light after her husband caught her enter-
taining men in their home. A dance hall girl named Belle Coine
nearly poisoned herself with toothache medicine that contained
liquid morphine. John O'Hara, who owned the Red Light at one
time, was not without a dark past himself. He had shot an innocent
bar patron in the face in a Park City saloon before taking over the
Red Light. Amazingly, the fellow survived the bullet that entered
his mouth and exited his ear.

The night of April 2, 1879, the Red Light Dance Hall became a
death hall. Trouble had been brewing all evening at the lively joint.
The Red Light was packed with at least twenty inebriated men by
10 p.m. Some couples on the dance floor had words with the
musicians, but things calmed down without violence. Calm did not
prevail for long as several men got into a tiff and almost came to
blows. This scene replayed over and over that evening with harsh
words spoken all the way around.

House manager Jackson "Jack" Jones was working the bar with
his barkeep and both were staying mighty busy. Jack was a 52-year-
old professional gambler from Texas. He came to Colorado in 1859
and, according to the *Fairplay Flume*, April 3, 1879, "had followed the
business of a gambler, dance house proprietor and bar-keeper [and]
[L]ike most true gamblers, he was very gentlemanly in deportment."

One of the revelers was Frank Jones (no relation to Jack), a 29-
year-old local bartender. A large man, he had worked in saloons in

Alma and Fairplay; both saloons had been the scenes of murders (See Chapters 25 and 29). At the end of a dance with an attractive young lady, Frank's good spirits got the best of him, and he hopped up to sit on the bar counter. Frank and Jack immediately had words, and it seemed to bystanders that an old grudge was being played out between the two. Jack threatened to "shoot him off" if Frank ever sat on the bar again. He went further and told the crowd that he would shoot the next man who tried to get up on the counter.

At that moment, Sheriff John Ifinger came into the saloon and ordered the two to stop their disturbance since a crowd had gathered to watch the anticipated fisticuffs. The men obliged. Frank pretended nothing had happened. The crowd once again relaxed, and Jack started taking drink orders.

As it turned out, the dispute was not over for Frank. He spun around and shot Jack Jones in the chest at close range as Jack stood behind the counter. Jack cried out, "Don't shoot anymore, I am a dead man!" Frank fired three more times before Sheriff Ifinger grabbed his arm to stop him. Ifinger collared the miscreant and marched him toward the door by the scruff of his neck.

Suddenly, the assistant barkeeper popped up from behind the counter and fired at Frank. He missed and almost hit the sheriff. Ifinger left the dance hall with his prisoner unscathed and headed for the county jail.

Jack was taken to a separate room in the dance hall where he expired within five minutes. Central City's newspaper, the *Daily Register-Call*, dismissed Jack's death quickly, claiming he had once served prison time for horse theft in Colorado Springs and that he had also been in trouble in Denver. "His end is not much regretted here," the paper sniffed.

Frank's court case is best described as a miscarriage of justice. Bond was set at only $500, an insult since the charge was premeditated murder. He made bail within thirty minutes and was back out on the streets for a month before his trial started on May 1. Jury selection was difficult, and the star witness, Sheriff Ifinger, was never called to the stand. The only testimony came from the Red Light patrons, who swore the shooting was in self-defense, a popular alibi at the time. On April 10, 1879, the *Flume* editorialized: "All of the witnesses called were of that class who believe in the principle that a live man is always better than a dead one. Their testimony showed but one side. . . . The trial was farcical."

Frank Jones was found guilty of manslaughter and received a seven-year prison sentence.

Four years later, on April 26, 1883, Frank received a full pardon from Governor James Grant based on the facts that he had served a large portion of his sentence and he was in poor health. The third reason, as reported in the *Flume*, was,

> That the conviction of the prisoner was largely the result of an excited state of feeling in Park county at the time in regard to the prevalence of crime, which public feeling operates strongly and unfairly against the accused.

Thomas Bowen, the sentencing judge, was among those who signed the petition for pardon. So much for frontier justice.

THE MURDER SITE TODAY

The Red Light Dance Hall was located at the west end of Front Street in Fairplay. It burned to the ground in 1883, after the dance hall had closed and the building was being used to store hay. Stroll down Fairplay's Front Street and imagine a raucous good time and noisy laughter emitting from the old saloons in days gone by or visit the South Park City Museum for a realistic look at western history.

The Fairplay Hotel, where J. J. Hoover shot and killed Thomas Bennett. *Courtesy Park County Local History Archives #1678. Source: South Park Historical Foundation.*

Chapter Twenty-Five

A COURTHOUSE LYNCHING
1880

J ohn Hoover's lynching from the Park County Courthouse
window in April 1880 is one of Park County's most often told
crime stories. His trial was part of the District Count term that
was called "the court that never adjourned" in an article in the 1966
Westerners Brand Book, and "the court that is still in recess" in a
Frontier Times magazine article in November 1972. The gruesome
event has been re-told in several "true story" western magazines,
numerous newspaper articles, and several books.

The story is retold here because Hoover's fate affected the
sentences of two other Park County murderers—Cicero C. Sims
and John W. Laughlin. It also helps modern readers understand the
climate in the county that contributed to Hoover's demise and the
problems that inconsistent sentencing created.

Little is known about John J. Hoover's early life other than he
was born in New York around 1842. The only physical description of
him comes from newspapers on his sentencing day, April 29, 1880.
The *Fairplay Flume* noted that he was "rotund and ruddiness on
every feature." Hoover was married to Euphrasia S. Maxey (or
Maxcy) of Augusta, Maine, a good friend of Horace Tabor's first wife,
Augusta, who was from the same town. Hoover married well.
Euphrasia's brother was Ward Maxey, who was later elected mayor
of Fairplay. Ward and Euphrasia had four other siblings, including
Nathaniel P. Maxcy, who came west with the Tabors in 1859.

Hoover first came to Leadville in the 1860s, when the mining
area was called Oro City. Horace "HAW" Tabor and family moved
over the range from Oro City to Buckskin Joe in 1861. By 1866,

Hoover had joined them, according to that year's U. S. Tax Assessment Lists. He was listed as a miner in Buckskin Joe, where he owned $297 worth of property taxed at $14.95.

On October 1, 1867, Hoover and his partners made an exciting discovery when they found "free gold" in a quartz vein between California and Eureka Gulches above Leadville; they named the strike the Five-Twenty Lode. The following year, Hoover discovered another lode and christened it the American Flag. It was located just east of the famous Printer Boy Mine where the first gold strike was discovered in Leadville. By 1871, Hoover was also involved with the Printer Boy. His streak of good luck broke on January 28, 1871, when he fell sixty-five feet down the shaft of the Printer Boy. His serious injuries were noted in the February 7, 1871, *Rocky Mountain News*:

> From a letter received Saturday from Oro City by Mr. H.A.W. Tabor, we learn that John Hoover met with a very serious accident a few days since by falling down the shaft of the printer Boy lode, a distance of sixty-five feet, crippling him severely.

Hoover's injuries would be the basis for his plan to plead insanity at his 1879 trial.

Hoover recovered quickly. A few months after his accident, he was superintendent of the Printer Boy.

When silver was found on Mount Bross near Alma in 1872, John and Euphrasia moved back to Fairplay, where John purchased a liquor and cigar store in partnership with Ward Maxcy. Hoover also owned the BonTon Saloon and the Cabinet Billiard Parlor in Fairplay, but sold the latter to John Nygent (aka Nugent) in August 1878. His ownership in the billiard parlor was contested when the mortgage holder, Thomas Smitham, filed a complaint against Hoover in August 1878, alleging the debtor had made no payments on $400 that he borrowed in December 1877. Hoover signed a promissory note to pay back the full amount by June. Ironically, Smitham's attorney was Elisha Bass, who prepared Hoover's criminal defense the following year but died before he could defend the suspect in court.

Hoover may not have reaped enough gold in Leadville or Buckskin Joe to support himself and his wife for he was also in debt to Ward Maxcy for $1,000. In the end, Maxcy had to collect his money through a lawsuit.

Once established in Fairplay, Hoover became a Fairplay Town Board trustee. The board's first order of business was to issue an order ". . . that the town ditch should be opened at once and kept open during the season," as printed in the *Fairplay Flume* on March 6, 1879.

The Fairplay town ditches were man-made dirt troughs and vital to the town. The water source was Beaver Creek northwest of Fairplay that brought fresh water from river headwaters to the town. Residents scooped a bucketful or two of water at a time for personal use, and if more was needed, a temporary dam could be constructed to fill larger containers. Sometimes questionable methods were used, such as cramming gunny sacks and old rags in the water stream.

The newspaper detailed the ongoing ditch problems, including mention of a "drove of swine rooting up the ditch banks" in 1879 and that a Fairplay hotel had washed its spittoons in the ditch water. On October 21, 1880, the *Flume* editor appealed, "How long oh, how long, are we to be without decent and proper water facilities?"

Within this context, John McLain, the proprietor of the Fairplay House on Front Street near the Hoover home, hired Thomas Bennett. McLain paid Bennett to clean out the ditch that ran opposite his hotel because it was flooding the Hoover's personal property. Hoover had recently complained that the ditch was a "menace" and threatened to shut it off. However, the April 5, 1879, *Rocky Mountain News* opined that the water overflow was not enough to harm Hoover's property.

Bennett was young man from Avoca, Iowa. He had worked as a stagecoach driver but was now out of a job and boarding at the Fairplay hotel. Bennett worked on the clean-up for most of March 31, 1879, and for a few minutes the next day before returning to the Fairplay House, where he lingered in the office. Propping his elbows on the long wooden counter, the young man leisurely perused the hotel register. Two customers, a Mr. H. Dice and Joseph McCarter, were lounging in the office, chatting and reading.

Around 2 p.m., Hoover downed some liquid courage, and strode to the hotel. Interrupting the pleasant scene, Hoover angrily announced to Bennett, "I own the house and lot and I'm not going to have my family imposed upon!" For added emphasis, Hoover stuck his revolver, a double-action 38 caliber, six-chamber Colt, in the fellow's face. Surprised, Bennett immediately moved to the end of the counter, exclaiming, "Hold on, I don't want any trouble, nor I don't want to impose on anyone."

Before the last word was out of his mouth, Hoover took one step back and shot Bennett in the chest; the ball traveled through his body and dropped on the floor nearby. "I am shot!" cried Bennett, throwing his arms up across his chest. He fell forward onto the hotel counter, then staggered backward and sank to the floor. The commotion brought the dining room girls and Mrs. McLain, to the dining room door for a peek. "Go back in there, God-damn you and shut the door, the whole lot of you!" Hoover shouted. The women scurried back into the kitchen.

Bennett made a feeble effort to get up, but Hoover wasn't quite done with him. In an act of disrespect and outrage, Hoover covered him with his pistol and cursed at the poor man: "Get up! Get up, you God damned son-of-a-bitch and I will give it to you again!" Dice stepped up and smacked Hoover on the arm, "Let the man alone, you've already done enough." With this, Hoover stood still for about half a minute, then turned and walked out.

Maybe Hoover thought he was enforcing the town board's recent order to open all the town ditches by telling Bennett to stop his work on the ditch. The *Rocky Mountain News*, September 10, 1879, alleged Hoover's problem was "stimulant use." John and Euphrasia had buried their only child, four-month-old Louisa, just months earlier. Perhaps the events converged and ignited his temper against a young man who was simply doing what he was hired to do—clean out a ditch. The *Rocky Mountain News* glibly summed up by saying Hoover's "liver was out of order" that day.

Witnesses carried the victim upstairs to an empty room, and someone went to flag down Sheriff Ifinger. The sheriff proceeded to Cabinet Billiards where Hoover, at his wife's urging, was waiting to turn himself in. "You can consider me your prisoner," the shooter said quietly as the sheriff walked in. The lawman escorted his new prisoner to the jail located in the courthouse basement.

In the meantime, Bennett gave his last statement. He declared he had not quarreled with Hoover and never threatened him. He had no idea why he was shot.

A messenger was dispatched to find Fairplay's Dr. Ramey, but he was attending another patient twenty-five miles south at Buffalo Springs. The doctor arrived back in town at 9 p.m., only to find that Bennett had expired. Ramey's medical deposition was therefore short: "Bennett is dead and to the best of my judgment, he died from the effects of the shot."

The coroner wanted to convene an inquest, but the jury members were tied up with the inquest investigating the murder of Jack Jones by Frank Jones just hours earlier in Fairplay (See Chapter 24). Two days later, the inquest was held and determined: "Thomas Bennett came to his death by a pistol shot on the afternoon of the 1st day of April, A.D. 1879 in Fairplay, Park County, Colorado and that said shot was fired by John J. Hoover feloniously."

Hoover appeared in court April 3, 1879, for his preliminary examination and was ordered back to jail to await the grand jury's action. The grand jury convened one month later when Judge Thomas M. Bowen arrived in town, accompanied by his wife and a court stenographer. During Colorado's early statehood, District Court was held by circuit judges who held court at pre-appointed times. The state legislature designated two court terms per year for each county with Park County's set for the third Monday in May and October. The sheriff took Hoover and murder suspect Frank Jones to Denver for safekeeping to await their next court dates.

Hoover's case was fraught with continuances that ultimately contributed to his demise. The trial, originally scheduled for one month after the shooting, was postponed because three key defense witnesses could not be located. Their testimony was vital to Hoover's insanity plea, a legal ploy his attorney planned to use based on his mine fall injuries and the subsequent change in personality and behavior. Court documents stated that he was "subject quite frequently to such fits of insanity and mental derangement."

The missing witnesses were Assyria "Cy" Hall, John Nugent, and Hugh Young. All three knew the defendant well enough to notice a personality change after the mine accident. Hoover was left sitting in a Denver jail for an entire year while his attorney tried to locate the witnesses. The trial was now set for the spring 1880 term of District Court with the same Judge Bowen. In another twist, Hoover's attorney,

Elisha Bass, died two and a half weeks before the trial was set to begin. Bass's partner, J. Q. Charles of Denver, took over the case, but Bass's trial preparation was lost on Charles. The new counsel ordered subpoenas for the witnesses and filed for another continuance in order to prepare for the trial.

The Park County sheriff brought Hoover back to Fairplay on Sunday, April 25, 1880, the day before his trial, along with Sims and Laughlin. In an effort to act on the languishing case, the court and the district attorney allowed Hoover to change his plea from "not guilty" to "manslaughter," which carried a lesser sentence. It was the most expedient way to dispose of the case, and due to Hoover's already lengthy incarceration, no one considered that the crime was still on the minds of the Fairplay citizenry.

Before commencing Hoover's trial, Judge Bowen had a number of other cases to hear. Finally, it was John Hoover's turn for his day in court. "Let the prisoner stand up." These words were the judge's first words according to the April 29, 1880, edition of the *Fairplay Flume*. The standing-room-only crowd in the courthouse was already agitating for a guilty verdict and a long prison sentence. The judge, however, launched into a quick description of the plea agreement and imposed a sentence of "eight years' service in the penitentiary at Canon City."

Grumblings could be heard in the courtroom and someone allegedly muttered, "Bring a rope!" The townsfolk were tired of the nonsense. Because of the crowds' agitation, Sheriff Ifinger placed two guards at the jail. In spite of staying up until approximately 2 a.m. himself, he was not terribly concerned about a lynching. He should have been.

In the dead of night, approximately twenty men with their faces covered quietly gathered. According to the sheriff's later deposition, the group knocked on his door. When he asked who was there, the muffled reply was: "We want to see the sheriff. We will break your door down if you don't come out."

Mrs. Ifinger opened the door and the men surged in and surrounded the sheriff. "They used me pretty roughly and pointed a six-shooter at me," the lawman later testified. His family was terrified.

The mob demanded the keys to the jail. Ifinger refused to turn over the keys. At this, the group demanded the keys from the sheriff's wife. When she too refused, they entered and searched the house, and found the keys to the inner cells.

The group then silently approached the nearby courthouse. According to jail guards Walter Taylor and James Beach, at 3:10 a.m. five or six masked men, revolvers in hand, ordered "Give us your arms." Taylor and Beach surrendered and the men walked out, instructing the two to remain in place. Ten minutes later, two of the masked men came back into the jail office, demanding the keys (presumably to the outer door), but the guards did not have them.

Not waiting for keys, others of the vigilante group were breaking down the outer jail door! Once inside the jail, they broke open the cell door, ripping it off its very hinges, even though they had found the keys in Ifinger's home. Hoover tried to raise an alarm by throwing his shoe and a tin can through his cell window. He did succeed in breaking the glass, and he "raised a shrill cry which aroused many, but was not understood nor heeded." Collaring him, two of the "lynch men" forced a rope over his head and around his neck, creating a makeshift leash. "Must I die like a dog?" wailed Hoover. The reply from one of the masked men was, "Bennett died like a dog."

The mob dragged Hoover out of his cell and into the night. Hustling him up the front steps of the courthouse, the anonymous group made quick of their work according to the account on the *Rocky Mountain News*, April 29, 1880.

> The end of the rope was then thrown to the upper story and placed around the stone pillar that divides the window. In less time than it takes to relate it, and without giving time to the trembling culprit to say a word, he was hauled up until his head nearly reached the upper window and the rope secured.

Hoover was not even allowed the courtesy of any final words.

The vigilantes were never identified. The sheriff and Deputy Sheriff Greene cut Hoover's body down in the bright moonlight, wrapped it in blankets, and carried it into the jail. The coroner's inquest held in the jail that night concluded, "John J. Hoover came to his death by being hung from the neck by a party of masked men and to the jury unknown." Taylor was instructed to untie the rope from the neck and hand it over as evidence.

Hoover was lynched from the window above the staircase in the front of the court-house. *Courtesy Becky Young, Becky Young Photography*

Although legend has it that the judge found a coiled noose on his desk when he entered his courthouse office the next morning, he remained in town long enough to complete the trial of Cicero Sims that same morning. Supposedly, the court officers had been threatened to bring in a conviction on Sims or things would go hard on them. Frank Jones also had his trial but the date is unclear; this resulted in a murder conviction as well.

The vigilantes posted a warning sign written in imitation blood outside the post office building. It read in part:

Citizens

We have organized to make this

A country of safety!

105 men, brave and true, in this country alone have

sworn to enforce the laws and punish MURDERERS.

We mean business!

We are carefully watching three persons

In Fairplay

Who are meddling with our affairs!

If one single member of our organization

Is arrested or tampered with for the

Hanging of Hoover, the MURDERER,

These suspected parties will share Hoover's

Fate without a moment's delay!

We mean to protect ourselves and society

And will spare neither Man nor Woman

Who dares to interfere in the slightest

Degree with our efforts to punish

Beware of the Vengeance of the Vigilantes!

Do not tear this down.

The "new" Park County Courthouse is shown in this late 1890s photo. *Courtesy Park County Local History Archives # 3341. Source: South Park Historical Foundation, photo by Dr. C. Scott*

At learning that "three people" were being watched, the court stenographer, the judge, and his wife, who had been quite worried all along, beat a hasty retreat out of town. Folks arriving at the courthouse for legal proceedings the following day were dismayed to find the officials had left without formally closing the court's spring session. This early close of court has been dubbed "the court that never adjourned." John W. Laughlin's murder trial had to be continued until the October term of court, possibly saving his life.

The *Fairplay Flume* of May 6, 1880, scolded the retreating entourage, stating:

> They became frightened unnecessarily and no doubt they imagined themselves in actual danger, but had they been nervy they would have stood at their post of duty in any event, instead of ingloriously "skipping" the town as they did last Thursday afternoon, leaving an unfinished docket and a record for timorousness . . . and all the excuse that his

friends can offer is that Judge Bowen left on account of his wife's fears.

One month later, Bowen resigned his judgeship on the grounds that he was "overworked and in bad health." Exiting the judicial scene allowed Bowen to pursue his political ambitions and his mining ventures. Both paid huge dividends. The flamboyant judge was elected to the United States Senate in 1882. His Rio Grande County mining claims made him a rich man. He estimated his wealth at $5,000,000 in the *Rocky Mountain News*, October 21, 1881.

Euphrasia Hoover remained in Fairplay, held her head high, and opened a millinery shop that she ran with a friend until she remarried a mine superintendent in 1883. Augusta Tabor remained a steadfast friend to Euphrasia. When Augusta died in 1895, Euphrasia was $856 in debt to her.

THE COURTHOUSE TODAY

The original Park County courthouse was built in 1874 and is listed on the National Register of Historic Places. It is located at 418 Main Street in Fairplay. For a time, the building housed the Fairplay Public Library. The jail was in the lower level or basement until a new jail was built in October 1880. The 1880 jail is a small brick building adjacent to historic courthouse building.

McLaughlin's Livery, where Mrs. Fitzgerald found the rifle she brandished as she chased her husband's murderer. McLaughlin's was an important business in Fairplay in the 1800s because it served as the McLaughlin Stage Line headquarters. *Courtesy Park County Local History Archives #1547. Source: South Park Historical Foundation.*

Chapter Twenty-Six

A WIDOW in HOT PURSUIT
1881

W hat a sight it must have been to see the Widow Fitzgerald chasing George Tattersall, her husband's alleged murderer, down the streets of Fairplay with a loaded rifle, skirts a' flying! This tragicomedy happened in the spring of 1881. Tattersall was a short and rather plain-looking Englishman, who took off at a dead run as the furious widow chased him.

Where did she get the rifle? She snatched it from McLaughlin's Livery Stable, where it was kept propped against a wall. The distraught widow left the courtroom and rushed into the livery office and grabbed the rifle, swearing vengeance on the man who had just been acquitted of murdering her husband, Lawrence, eleven months earlier.

This was not the first time Mrs. Fitzgerald had tried to get even with her husband's slayer. The scrape had started on April 12, 1880, in Leadville, just over the Mosquito Mountain Range from Fairplay. Mr. and Mrs. Fitzgerald lived in a cabin near their mining claim, the Bringham & Beecher Lode, in the rich Leadville Mining District. Fitzgerald had staked a mining claim next to several of Tattersall's claims. The latter tried "jumping" the front portion of the Fitzgerald's location by clearing the ground to build a cabin. When Mrs. Fitzgerald saw what Tattersall was doing, she ran out of her cabin and ordered him to stop. He stopped long enough to swear at her, then continued his work on the cabin site.

A few days later, Tattersall showed up with thirty logs to begin building his cabin. Lawrence Fitzgerald confronted him and tried to move one of the logs away. Words were exchanged followed by blows. Tattersall pulled out his six-shooter and fired three times. The last shot killed Fitzgerald.

Tattersall hightailed it down the street, but not alone. Thirty to forty men ran after him. A reporter for the *Daily Register-Call* newspaper, April 13, 1880, claimed the crowd swelled to two hundred with only one thing on their minds—lynching the murderer. Tattersall's neck was literally saved when a law officer intervened and threw him in jail.

The prisoner first appeared in the Lake County courtroom on February 3, 1881, nearly a year later. Fitzgerald's widow took a seat in the courtroom early that morning, even though the case was not scheduled for a hearing until noon. After listening intently to the proceedings, she left the room and stood near the front entrance to the courthouse, where she would have a clear shot when officers escorted Tattersall down the stairs. The *Rocky Mountain News*, February 5, 1881, reported what happened next.

> A few who were watching the woman in black from the end of the hall saw her suddenly thrust her hand beneath her shawl and, an instant later, caught the bright gleam of a revolver barrel. The guards and prisoner neared and springing forward, she drew the weapon and thrust it into the murderer's face. At the same fraction of time, one of the officers, realizing the situation, seized her arm and wrenched the revolver from her grasp.

Mrs. Fitzgerald wasn't done yet. The Lake County judge ordered a change in venue, and the trial was moved to Fairplay. Two months later the suspect and the Lake County sheriff boarded the train for Fairplay. Mrs. Fitzgerald sat directly behind the two, revolver in hand. The sheriff must have put a stop to any intentions to shoot Tattersall because the prisoner arrived in Fairplay for trial. Mrs. Fitzgerald's hopes for revenge now lay with the Fairplay court. On May 5, 1881, following several days of testimony, the jury deliberated through the night, and returned a verdict of not guilty. The courtroom spectators gasped when the verdict was announced.

The defendant stepped out of the courthouse a free man, but by no means safe. Mrs. Fitzgerald left the courtroom, grabbed the rifle in the livery, and chased Tattersall through the streets of Fairplay.

Later, she admitted to a *Flume* reporter that her intention was indeed to do away with the man who killed her husband.

Two months later, Tattersall was still skittish. A Lake County sheriff's deputy, who was visiting in Fairplay, saw Tattersall walking down the street and called to greet him. Tattersall turned around, trembling. When the lawman asked how he was doing he replied, "I will never stand another trial and prefer death to getting into the wife's presence."

THE LIVERY BARN TODAY

Stroll into the Old Red Barn, an antique and western memorabilia store on the corner of Front and Fifth Streets in Fairplay. This was originally McLaughlin's Livery Stable where a grieving wife found a rifle and the point from where she chased her husband's killer down Front Street.

THE COURTHOUSE TODAY

The original Park County courthouse was built in 1874 and is on the National Register of Historic Places. It is located at 418 Main Street, and until 2013, housed the Fairplay Public Library. The jail was originally in the lower level or basement. A new jail adjacent to the courthouse was built in October 1880. The small brick jail is not open to the public at the time of this writing.

The Park County Jail, located just west of the courthouse in Fairplay, housed the county's miscreants. Constructed in 1880, it still stands today. *Courtesy Christie Wright*

Chapter Twenty-Seven

SHOOTING UP the TOWN of FAIRPLAY
1879 & 1908

B eing a Colorado lawman in the 1880s wasn't easy. Small
towns such as Fairplay, Alma, and Como typically had a town
marshal, who was either appointed by the local Town Board
or voted in through a general election. Salaries were modest; Park
County paid $90 a month in 1893 and presumably less in the pre-
ceding years. A marshal's duties included keeping the peace, serving
warrants, and enforcing town ordinances among other responsibili-
ties. These ordinances typically included petty offenses such arrest-
ing the drunk and disorderly, locking up cheating gamblers, and
running vagrants, or "vags", off private property.

The April 24, 1879, *Fairplay Flume* gives an idea of what the
town of Fairplay was like during the early years and why there was
a need for law officers:

> The practice of firing guns and pistols inside the corporate
> limits of Fairplay has become of such frequent occurrence
> as to be classed a nuisance and should receive some atten-
> tion from the city guardians. Some restraint against carrying
> concealed weapons is also earnestly expected from our
> town council at a very early day by all few abiding citizens.

SHOT IN THE BACK AND LIVED TO TELL
1879

On July 3, 1879, a railroad worker named John Sweeney was lying
around the Sullivan boarding house in Fairplay, where he lived.
Earlier that day, he made an "improper display of his person," and

the proprietor booted him out into the street whereupon he began quarreling with several local roughs.

Town Marshal Henry Seymour and Deputy Sheriff Greene arrested Sweeney. Deputy Greene left to sort out another disturbance, and the marshal headed toward the jail with his charge. En route, Sweeney bolted and ran. He got as far as McLaughlin's Livery Stable a few blocks away. Seymour fired two warning shots, which merely aggravated Sweeney, who threw a handful of stones at the marshal in retaliation. When Sweeney began running again, the marshal fired and the bullet found its mark in the ruffian's backside.

Sweeney was taken back to his boarding house where the attending doctor pronounced the injury would be fatal. A few weeks later however, a more sober Sweeny was on the mend, notwithstanding a permanent paralysis on his right side. The doctor had probed deep into his flesh for the bullet with no luck. That experience probably served as a deterrent from future antics. He carried the bullet in his backside the rest of his life.

ONE MARSHAL'S "HIGH LONESOME"
1908

Sometimes the frontier lawmen found themselves on the wrong side of the law. Such was the case on a Sunday night in March 1908 when Fairplay Town Marshal Nat Tryon was, in the words of the *Fairplay Flume* later that week, "out on a high lonesome" and "crazy drunk." The marshal played cards until four in the morning when a dispute arose between the marshal and another card player named Erik Erickson. The newspaper theorized that Tryon had a grudge against Erickson and in his drunken stupor had wanted to kill him.

Tryon pulled out his gun for effect at one point in the game and was quickly disarmed by his more sober cronies at the table. They returned his gun to him after he promised to behave and go home when the group disbanded. Upon leaving the saloon, instead of behaving, he fired a shot into the upstairs of Cohen's Hardware Store on Front Street. Several miners, including Erickson, boarded in Cohen's hardware. Erickson was in his room and narrowly escaped Tryon's bullet as it zoomed past his head. Two weeks later, on March 27, 1908, the *Flume* reported that the dispute may have started when Erikson, "either held five aces or failed to contribute to the 'kitty'."

The marshal was charged with disturbing the peace and entered a "not guilty" plea during his day in court. His wild streak did not end there. A few months later, Tryon was charged with being drunk and disorderly and mistreating his family. Oddly enough, Tyron was struck by lightning near his own home the following summer, perhaps a warning from above to behave. On November 5, 1909, Marshal Tryon pled guilty to the drunk and disorderly charges. The judge gave the marshal a choice of "ten"—ten days' jail time or a ten-dollar fine. He paid the fine rather than serve jail time in his own jurisdiction.

THE SHOOTING SITES TODAY

John Sweeney was shot by Officer Henry Seymour opposite McLaughlin's Livery Stable. Located at the corner of Front and Fifth Streets, the building is now the Old Red Barn, a store selling antique and western memorabilia.

Cohen's Hardware store was a brick building on Front Street in Fairplay. Buildings of the same era as the hardware store still stand on Front Street, which is lined with shops.

This undated photo of the St. Nicholas Hotel in Alma shows it bedecked for a Fourth of July celebration. Sims ate breakfast in the hotel unguarded on the morning of his first court appearance, January 29, 1880. *Courtesy Park County Local History Archives #1740. Source: South Park Historical Foundation.*

Chapter Twenty-Eight

SIMS' SWING
1880

Sylvester "Cicero" Sims (also spelled Simms) was the youngest of nine children born to Benjamin Miles Sims and Mary Ann Prince in 1861 in Ducktown (Polk County), Tennessee. Benjamin was a Baptist preacher, who died within a year of Cicero's birth. Mary died three years later in 1864, leaving the children to fend for themselves. Three older brothers, William, George, and Columbus, may have stepped in and looked after young Cicero, just as the latter two would do on his last day on earth on July 24, 1880.

Polk County was known for the Burra Burra Copper Mine, discovered in 1843, where Cicero went to work as a child. Sims told the *Rocky Mountain News* on July 22, 1880, "When I got big enough, they set me to work in the copper mines at Ducktown and I stayed there for a long time." There were no child labor laws in place in Tennessee at that time, and the work was strenuous and difficult. Laborious mine work at such a young age may have been the source of Sims' stoicism that would come in so handy after his arrest in Colorado.

Following in his brothers' footsteps, Cicero crossed the great prairie to Colorado in 1878. Two of the brothers had settled in Breckenridge, where George ran a lodging house and worked at Park County's prosperous Dolly Varden Mine on Mount Bross. Columbus worked at the Boston & Colorado Works at Argo in north Denver.

Cicero's legal escapades were reported in several Colorado newspapers. He pulled a gun on Fairplay brewery owner Joe Summer in April 1879, without consequence. Sherriff Ifinger merely ordered him to put his gun away. And he may well have been involved in a shooting skirmish in Malta, just outside Leadville, in June 1879. Rumors of more serious crimes committed by young Sims were false according to his brother George, who tried to dispel them in an open letter printed in the February 5, 1880, *Fairplay Flume*. George denied that Cicero assaulted a Kansas saloon keeper who attacked Cicero with a poker and permanently scarred his face. Furthermore, George patently denied that his younger brother had killed a man in Grenada, Colorado, in 1874.

Shortly after settling in Alma, Sims met a Danish miner named John Jansen, who was sixteen years his senior. The two lived together for several weeks in Jansen's cabin, with Jansen providing the food and Sims doing the cooking. Jansen worked at Alma's Boston & Colorado Works and also did odd jobs. According to the *Flume*, January 29, 1880, he was "an industrious, hard-working man without an enemy and with many friends. He had secured several excellent mining claims on one of which a shaft of sixty feet was sunk."

On the night of January 25, 1880, Jansen and Sims played cards at Lew Link's saloon on Buckskin Street and ate together, then stepped outside onto the sidewalk. Perhaps the frigid night air sparked the horseplay, but the friends began sparring, joking, and knocking each other's hats off, a common game at the time. The *Rocky Mountain News* described the scene in a July 24, 1880, article. Jansen knocked Sims' hat a few feet away. Sims turned to Jansen and, according to the article, these words led to the shooting.

"You pick that hat up!"

"Oh, no," replied Jansen, "That wouldn't be fair. When you knocked my hat off, I picked it up myself both times."

The refusal stung Simms, and he became angry in a moment.

"Are you going to pick up my hat?" he fiercely demanded.

"No," quietly responded Jansen.

"You'd better do it," urged Simms in an imperious way. "If you don't, you're a dead man! G-d d-n you! I've a notion to give it to you anyhow."

Suiting the action to the word, Simms pulled his revolver, took aim and fired. Jansen fell heavily to the ground. The ball had entered the brain just between the eyes, and its effect had killed him instantly.

Once the deed was done, the culprit backed away, holding the smoking gun while horrified onlookers rushed to the victim. Some ran for the doctor while others started in hot pursuit of the offender, who had darted into the nearby forest. Twenty citizens were on his tail. They had no trouble following his footprints in the snow until the tracks led back to town and mixed with all the other footprints.

A messenger was dispatched to Fairplay to alert Sheriff John Ifinger, who arrived in Alma late that same evening and renewed the search. He called off the manhunt at 3 a.m. so the volunteers could rest.

Early the next morning, Ifinger telegraphed the Rocky Mountain Detective agency, Denver's Chief of Police William R. Hickey, and sheriffs in the neighboring counties with a description of the alleged murderer. Frustrated townsfolk authorized the president of the Alma Town Board, J. G. Brooks, to issue a $500 reward, and the following description was published in the *Rocky Mountain News* on January 29, 1880, and sent to all state law enforcement offices:

> Simms is about five feet six inches tall, slender, very light complexion, large staring blue or gray sunken eyes, high cheek bones, square chin, small mouth, moustache hardly perceptible and no whiskers, scar on underside of right jaw resembling a cut or burn. When he left Alma he had on a pair of fine boots with small heels, black hat, black half-frock coat and light pants. Said Simms is a native of east Tennessee.

A coroner's inquest conducted by Justice of the Peace Robert F. Neuhaus, concluded: "The deceased came to his death by a pistol shot from a weapon in the hand of C.C. Simms." Jansen's burial in the Buckskin Cemetery on January 26 was attended by his friends. No family members could be contacted as the names of his Denmark relatives were unknown.

As for Sims, the outlaw showed up in Denver on January 28,

1880, at a boardinghouse called the Columbus House at Sixteenth and Wazee Streets. With the murderer's physical description available to law enforcement agencies and reward money on Sims' head, proprietor Jacob Daniels was keeping a keen eye out. He was soon rewarded.

Sims arrived after the cold, ninety-mile journey at 1 a.m., with his feet badly swollen from frostbite and complaining of the winter temperatures. After all his cleverness in avoiding an Alma lynching, young Sims slipped up and signed the boarding house register, "Cicero Sims, Alma," in bold strokes.

Daniels noticed his new customer was wearing a pair of rough, ill-fitting cowhide boots and a warm brown coat. How Sims came into possession of these things is anyone's guess because when he absconded, he was wearing "fine boots" and a black coat. Did he hitch a wagon ride and trade clothes with a stranger or do something more devious, such as commit another murder?

After registering the exhausted stranger, Daniels stepped out on the streets and came upon Denver Police Chief Hickey and Officer H. C. Sherman near the corner of Blake and Fifteenth Streets. The two were talking over the enticing enticing reward money on Sims' head, which lawmen were allowed to collect in those days.

After listening for a minute, Daniels piped up and described the disheveled fellow who had checked in limping and rambling about the cold mountain temperatures. The lawmen were convinced they had their man. Daniels led the way up the creaking wooden stairs of the Columbus House to a large sleeping apartment. Six men slumbered in the barren room. Officer Sherman easily recognized Sims because he had questioned him only one month earlier about a Denver robbery. Lifting his lantern high by a narrow cot, the light illuminated Sims' peaceful visage, reposed in sleep. The *Rocky Mountain News* of July 24, 1880, gave a descriptive account:

> Pulling him by the shoulder he (Sherman) asked quickly,

> "Say Simms, what did you do with Jansen?"

> The sleeper awoke with a start and without realizing his position, replied:

"Oh, I don't know, I left him up at Alma," turned over and was about to again commit himself to the arms of the drowsy god, when he was lifted almost bodily out of bed and stood upon his legs in the middle of the room. As this was done, it was discovered that his feet were very badly swollen, having been frozen and it was with great difficulty that he continued to walk about.

He was allowed to dress and "when the order was given to march, his efforts to put them (his boots) on his swollen feet were painful to the spectators as well as himself."

The murder weapon was found in Sims' belongings.

The prisoner was taken directly to the Denver jail, which was technically the Arapahoe County jail, as Denver was part of Arapahoe County at that time. Sims remained there briefly until Denver Officer Weber transported him back to Alma on the Denver, South Park & Pacific Railroad for a preliminary examination in front of Judge Neuhaus the following morning, January 29. This was the same Justice of the Peace Neuhaus who had convened the coroner's inquest panel days earlier.

For whatever reasons, Officer Weber embellished the story of transporting the prisoner the last sixteen miles from Red Hill station in Park County to Alma. In 1880, Red Hill was the "end of track" for the Denver, South Park & Pacific Railroad. Passengers continued their travels by wagon and horseback. Weber claimed that an armed lynching party was waiting for them at both Red Hill and Fairplay, and that he had bundled Sims in a blanket and raced his wagon through the towns to avoid the mobs.

When Sheriff Ifinger heard Weber's yarns, he stepped in and gave the true story. In reality, the proprietor of Vestel House, one of Fairplay's boarding houses, met Weber and Sims at Red Hill and drove them into Alma for breakfast. Sims ate alone at the St. Nicholas Hotel without a guard. Ifinger asserted that only about six men even knew the prisoner was in town, and although there had been some hotheads talking a good game, no attempts at a lynching were made.

With rumors dispelled and the preliminary examination completed in front of Neuhaus, the sheriff escorted his charge back to

Denver, where Sims remained for almost three months until his trial date on April 25, 1880.

As was customary, Sims was kept in heavy iron shackles most of the time. A bright spot for him was frequent visits by the Reverend Charles Ferrari, a Jesuit priest and the assistant pastor at Denver's Sacred Heart Church. Ferrari seemed to have an especially positive influence on the inmate, teaching Sims the ways of the Lord, something Sims' siblings had written to the church and requested.

Father Ferrari was a revered man who had been born into Italian royalty. The *Denver Catholic Register* of June 11, 1914, named him a "pioneer priest of the West," and his predecessor described him as "an angel in private life." Father Ferrari went on to be the first priest to institute Mass at the Territorial Prison in Cañon City, Colorado.

At the end of April, Sims awaited Sheriff Ifinger's arrival at the jail as did two other prisoners from Park County—John J. Hoover and John W. Laughlin. Ifinger transported all three murder suspects to Fairplay for their day in court, no small undertaking since only one guard accompanied him. The prisoners were each scheduled to appear in Park County District Court the following morning for their respective trials. Only one of the three would keep his neck.

The outcome of Sims' trial was intricately tied to Hoover's sentence. Hoover appeared in court the day before Sims and was let off with a term of eight years in the penitentiary, thanks to a plea arrangement that allowed him to enter a guilty plea to manslaughter. As noted in Chapter 25, Hoover was lynched at 3 a.m. the morning of Sims' trial. After Hoover's demise, "one of the vigilantes took the trouble to go down among the cells and tell Simms that it was 'lucky for him that they did not have time to attend to his case, but that they would see him later.'" (*Fairplay Flume*, April 29, 1880). Sims provided the Flume with the only eyewitness account of the jail break-in by a vigilante.

In an article printed July 24, 1880, *Rocky Mountain News* reporter Benjamin Zalinger provided a vivid description of the courtroom atmosphere at Sims' trial.

> The trial of Simms was one of the most exciting ever witnessed in any court. . . . There was continued fear, in the

first place, that the mob would get him before the judicial examination should have been concluded and this in itself was no trifling matter. Everybody understood what mob law and a lynching meant at the hand of the outraged Park county people. Then the judge and jury and attorneys were notified in the most solemn and awful way that if the prisoner were freed, it would go hard with those who assisted toward that end. It is even said that when Judge Thomas Bowen reach the court room on the second day of the trial, he found a piece of new rope very neatly coiled up on his j udicial desk.

The hints, curious as they were, had the desired result and the parties to the trial, including the spectators in the lobby, were kept in a state of the greatest excitement and anxiety. . . . The jury returned a verdict of murder in the first degree after an absence from the court room of about an hour and a half.

When Judge Bowen inquired if the prisoner has anything to say why the sentence of the law should not be pronounced upon him, Sims answered quietly that he did not. The judge then imposed sentence:

Then it is the order of the Court that you be taken from the bar of the court by the sheriff of this county to the common jail, from whence you came, there to be kept in safe and secure custody until the 11th day of June next, and on the said 11th day of June, at the hour of one o'clock in the afternoon of that day, that the said sheriff take your body to some convenient place in the town of Fairplay, in Park county, and then and there that you hang by the neck until you be dead.

Another version claims the judge emphasized each word as he said, "until you are dead, dead, DEAD," his voice raising with each syllable.

That afternoon, when other court-goers climbed the steep spiral steps to conduct their legal business, they found only court clerk Michael J. Bartley present. The judge, district attorney, and court

stenographer had skipped town! The *Flume* chided the entourage for
lacking nerve, noting they should have remained in town despite the
warnings and that they were not in any danger. Later, some historians
referred to this incident as "the court that never adjourned." Because
Bowen left an unfinished docket, John Laughlin's case was continued
to the next term of court in October 1880.

Less than thirty days after Sims' trial, Bowen resigned his judgeship, claiming he was "overworked and in ill health," according to
the May 26 *Rocky Mountain News*. He then pursued his prosperous
mining claims, including one called Bowen's Bonanza and eventually
became a very wealthy man. Two years after chastising Bowen for
his quick exodus, the *Flume* endorsed Bowen for governor over
Horace Tabor.

After sentencing, Sims was taken again to Denver for safekeeping
and to await his June execution date. His attorney, the well-known
General Samuel E. Browne of Denver, filed several appeals with the
Colorado Supreme Court, which refused to grant a new trial. The
execution date was changed to July 2, 1880.

Nonplussed, Browne appeared before Governor Frederick Pitkin
on June 29, 1880, spending practically the entire day with him to
request clemency and a delay of sentence and to review all the trial
evidence. Browne claimed some evidence "had not been submitted
to the Supreme Court which should have weight in inducing the
executive to commute the sentence to imprisonment for life." After
a day's consideration, Pitkin tentatively decided against commutation, saying he would give his final decision at 9 p.m. on June 30.
Several of Sims' friends, a few reporters, and Browne gathered in
the governor's office that evening to await Pitkin's arrival.

The governor came in around 10 p.m., whereupon Browne
announced that he could produce a sworn statement from Judge
Bowen affirming that all the court participants were intimidated
by a mob, and therefore Sims' trial was unfair. Browne requested
thirty days to obtain the statement from Bowen. Furthermore, the
attorney claimed that Sims did not have an opportunity to request
a new trial because the judge vacated prematurely.

This worked. Pitkin granted a stay of execution until July 23,
1880. When Browne informed Sims of the second extension, a brief
spark of hope crossed the stoic young man's face, but his elation

was short-lived. The governor had communicated with the Colorado Supreme Court about a sentence commutation for Sims and, after a review by the justices, had been told that commutation was out of the question.

Browne left for southern Colorado to spend a week locating Thomas Bowen and obtaining the desired affidavit. He found the ex-judge working his mines in the Summitville Mining District in Rio Grande County. However, Bowen would only write a letter of recommendation for commutation. He did not spell out the vigilante intimidation or mention why he left town. In essence, Bowen refused to put his fears in writing.

Browne's train pulled into Denver two hours late, and he telegraphed his law partner, Captain Thomas G. Putnam, and asked him to arrange a meeting with the governor. But Pitkin had already issued a statement denying a commutation of sentence. Sims was doomed.

During his last night in jail, the condemned man wrote a letter to his older sister, Mary Matilda Ann "Tildia" Sims, that provided a glimpse into the anguished heart of a young man who appeared to be so cold. In the letter, he lamented his fate but realized it was the price he had to pay for being "crazed by drink." He reminisced about their parents and closed his letter, "Farewell forever."

On execution morning, Sims was awakened at 6:30, by Arapahoe County Sheriff Spangler to await Sheriff Ifinger's arrival. *Rocky Mountain News* reporter Benjamin Zalinger was also present. He had received permission to shadow Sims up until he walked onto the scaffold. He later provided a detailed, personal account of how the doomed man fared through the day. Denver photographer William G. Chamberlain, set up his photo-taking apparatus to capture a final portrait of Sims for the newspapers and to sell to the curious public. The inmate consented on the condition that a copy be sent with the letter he had written to his sister. Sims was shackled and escorted out onto the front jailhouse lawn where Chamberlain made the photograph.

Sims, Sheriffs Ifinger and Spangler, and three newspaper reporters went by carriage to the train station on Sixteenth Street. Sims was helped out of the carriage and onto the South Park train platform, his fettered feet clanging awkwardly. The lawmen and

reporters did what they could to shield him from a jeering crowd;
they seemed to have developed a newfound sympathy for him.
As the train slowly backed up to the platform to load passengers,
Ifinger and Spangler barked out dispersal orders to the crowd that
had gathered to gawk at the man who would soon die.

Zalinger detailed the lengthy train ride in his subsequent article.
Lunch specifics. After-dinner cigars. A kind Christian woman who
held Sims' hand, speaking softly to him about the Lord. When they
disembarked at Red Hill station, a four-horse wagon team with ten
heavily armed men were waiting, all orchestrated by Sheriff Ifinger.
The guards were necessary because three weeks earlier some of
Sims' sympathizers had thought he was aboard an incoming train
and gathered at Red Hill ready to attempt a rescue. The wagon was
loaded and quickly left and bump-bumped along the rutty road
into Fairplay.

The town was filled with people who had come to watch the
county's first and only legal execution. Curious folks strolled about
town, large groups gathered on the street corners to chat, and the
Western Union telegraph office hummed with excitement as tidbits
of news were sent from the office every few minutes. As the fatal
hour drew near, businesses closed in Fairplay and Alma, and even
the miners came down from the hills to witness the doomed man's
"launch into eternity."

Zalinger walked one-quarter mile east of the courthouse to the
scaffold and saw it had been desecrated by drawings and vulgarities
carved into the rough wood. On the trap door, someone had drawn
footprints and gouged, "Simms, here's where you put your foot in
it." Below the drop, there was a drawing of a hanged man and
underneath was written, "Simms, how do you like it?" Ifinger
ordered the marks be obliterated.

Elbowing his way through the crowds, Zalinger got to the jail in
time to observe George and Columbus Sims' tearful thirty-minute
reunion with their brother. Zalinger described the touching scene
in the *Rocky Mountain News*, July 24, 1880.

> The handshake of the brothers was strong and vigorous and
> as indications pointed, full of grief and woe. There was very
> little said; the interview between the three was mostly carried

out by manifestation of the limbs and features. But it was touching in the extreme. The younger of the two brothers, (George) who is next to the prisoner in age, was visibly affected and tears trickled down his face in rapid succession.

"Are you quite prepared to go?" they asked.

"Yes, I think I've done all I can," he (Sims) replied and as there was too much of agitation, jailer James Cole thought it best to terminate the interview.

The reporter was then allowed time with the prisoner, and Sims suddenly opened up:

> I haven't had a fair trial in this business and I don't think I ought to die today. Jansen and I were good friends and I had no more idea of shooting him than I have of flying this minute, I was drinking that day and maybe that helped the thing along. I never drank anything at all until I came to Colorado. If I had had money though, I would have been all right. If my people in Georgia [a brother and sister] could have given me any money, I wouldn't be here today.

As he teared up, Sims continued, "They wrote one letter, but they said they couldn't do anything for me. They said they were sorry, but they are poor and so couldn't give me any help."

Reverend Ferrari arrived after lunch and remained with Sims until the bitter end. The condemned had a deep fondness for the pastor, and many believed that Ferrari's religious instruction was the reason for Sims's calmness throughout his ordeal.

"Come, time's up," Sheriff Ifinger motioned after the heavy iron jail cell door was opened. Sims was lifted up into an awaiting wagon, once again surrounded by guards, their shooting irons cocked. Rumors of a last-minute rescue had forced the sheriff to send scouts into the forest earlier that day for miles around. The guards kept a close watch on the pines and aspen as the group drove to the awaiting gallows.

The wagon stopped, and the procession alighted and walked up the scaffold steps. Sims proceeded quickly, without any signs of anxiety, and sat in a chair on the platform, his eyes wandering.

Father Ferrari prayed in a low voice. The sky had clouded over, and thunder and rain were imminent, adding yet another layer of gloom to the afternoon's business. As Ifinger read the death warrant, loud claps of thunder began in booming succession as if announcing the impending death.

Sims heaved violently when the sheriff read the phrase, "hang by the neck until he is dead." But he soon regained his composure. Most of the ladies were now weeping in their handkerchiefs.

"The prisoner shall rise," instructed Ifinger, and Sims obeyed, ready to face the audience and his impending fate.

"Do you have anything to say as to why the death sentence should not be executed?" queried the lawman.

Sims spoke in a low tone that was hard for the crowd to hear, so Father Ferrari repeated the words for the crowd. "I don't know as I have much to say. I have my life taken and I do not think I have had a fair trial or a fair show, but I am willing to forgive all who had a hand in it, if they will forgive me. I hope the Lord will forgive me my sins."

Ferrari then knelt by the young man, said a prayer and give absolution to the prisoner. The hundreds of onlookers became nervous and agitated, whispering and swaying. The guards stepped up, bound Sims' arms and legs and placed the black head cap over his head.

Officials on the platform stepped back from the center area and at 1:19 p.m., the lever was pulled, the trap door flew open, and Sylvester Cicero Sims was dead declared dead at 1:35. His body was lowered into a coffin awaiting under the scaffold, with the rope still around his neck. The Fairplay townsfolk had purchased the coffin, which was built by the jail guard, to give Sims a proper burial, and he was laid to rest in the Fairplay cemetery later that day.

After the execution, Zalinger borrowed Ifinger's horse and galloped eight miles back to Red Hill station to catch the Denver train. The engineer held the train for forty-five minutes for him, which allowed the newsman to turn in his story by the deadline for the next day's exciting issue.

The aftermath of the hanging was considerable. The Central City *Daily Register-Call* newspaper printed a sensational story that reported the hanging did not kill Sims, that he was buried and then dug up after the crowd left the cemetery. The doctor who declared him dead was supposedly hired by the two brothers and that Sims was in on the plan all along, which explained the fearlessness he had shown that day. A Leadville stage driver swore he was held up and forced to pick up a sick man (Sims) and drive him over the range to Leadville. The group then allegedly ordered the driver to return to Fairplay, where he engaged many in his incredible story.

All the Denver papers, as well as the Flume, ran special sections the morning after the hanging, with "full and detailed particulars, which if fully written would make a 50-page pamphlet" (*Weekly Register-Call*, July 30, 1880). Editorials expressed varying viewpoints on capital punishment. While the *Rocky Mountain News* espoused a religious point of view and denounced executions, the *Fairplay Flume* took a different position on July 29, 1880:

> The first public execution in Park county is a thing of the past, but its wholesome influence still remains and will work a healthy sentiment among would-be transgressors of the law. Judge Lynch has presided at every past execution in the county.

The *Leadville Weekly Herald* on July 31, 1880, published a poem as part of the story:

> In the Town of Fairplay, 'Neath the Sun's Golden Rays,
> Sims, for his Crime, the Dread Penalty Pays.
> Resigned to His Fate, Abandoning All Hope,
> The Red-Handed Murderer Dies by the Rope.
> Expressing Regret, Laying on Whisky the Blame,
> He Walks to his Fate and Bravely "Dies Game."

Sims and John Jansen have lain within ten miles of each other for well over a century. Although their grave markers have long since disintegrated, their mark upon this county's history remains.

THE MURDER SITE TODAY

Cicero Sims shot his friend John Jansen in front of Lew Link's saloon in Alma, but the building no longer stands. The saloon was located in the center of town on Buckskin Street near the Alma Fire Station Museum.

THE EXECUTION SITE

The scaffold where Sims was executed by hanging was one-quarter mile west of the courthouse, up a slight incline, and in a cottonwood grove. The location is best viewed today from Platte View Drive, which dead ends in a cul-de-sac with private homes along the street. The gravel parking area in the cul-de-sac is for homeowners only. Do not trespass, but pause to look down on the town of Fairplay and imagine the calm prisoner and the throngs of people assembled for his execution on July 22, 1880.

This engraving was made of Sims the morning of his execution and published in the *Rocky Mountain News,* July 24, 1880. Reproductions of the engraving were later sold in Denver stores as souvenirs. He was the only man legally executed by Park County, the state took over capital punishment in 1890.

This structure was the Alma jail for a time. It was Alma's second jail, built after the jail from which Porter 'swung' was destroyed by fire. The historic building in the photograph no longer stands either. *Courtesy Park County Local History Archives. Source: South Park Historical Foundation.*

Chapter Twenty-Nine

COMMITTED, TRIED, and EXECUTED in ONE HOUR—1880

"**D**amn you—pull up your rope, boys!" William "Bill" J. Porter taunted, as he sucked in his last breaths through gritted teeth. It was the evening of March 22, 1880, and Bill knew in a few minutes he would be "performing on the tight-rope" from the ridgepole above the Alma jailhouse. Porter was about to become yet another object of 1800s summary justice in Park County.

What prompted the vigilante group to string up Bad Bill? That evening around seven o'clock, the local fifty-two-year-old tough guy had words with a young Irish miner named Thomas Carmody in the Marsh & Mullen Saloon. Carmody was described by his friends as "a man who would not have injured anyone." A disagreement arose about religion, whereupon Carmody stood up to leave, telling Porter, "Well, ye's don't like my talk and I will go out."

Carmody stepped out of the saloon. Porter followed muttering coarse words at him. "I don't know what you mean," the young miner replied politely, the last sentence he would ever utter. Porter pulled out his pistol and shot the miner point-blank in the chest.

The town marshal, Lew Link, was nearby and slugged Porter in the face, bringing him down instantly. The marshal then single-handedly dragged Porter to the jail as the streets filled with indignant locals, already determined to see justice done. Link probably knew what was coming, as this scenario had played out many times before in Colorado.

Fifty citizens followed Link to the jail. Some of the group wrested the keys from the marshal and wrangled their man from the jail and into the cold night air, Porter stood a "bloody but defiant spectacle," with blood running from where Link coldcocked him with a cane. Above him, the ridgepole of the little jail extended four feet directly over the jail door and would do just fine as the anchor for the hanging rope. Some wondered if it wasn't a devilish design of the jail's builder since it was seemingly perfect for that night's purpose. Porter appeared fearless, cursing the men before him as they gawked.

"What'er yer final requests?" hollered one fellow from the group.

"I have some money coming from the mine where I've been working, and I want $31 paid to Old Man Fuller at the Southern Hotel," Porter replied. To some familiar faces in the crowd, he spoke his final request: "Write to my folks and tell them I'm dead, but not that I was hanged." He also asked that his two young sons not be told of his true demise. The slipknot was laid on Porter's shoulder like a coiled snake poised to strike.

"You got anything further to say?" piped up another voice.

"Damn you—pull up your rope, boys," was his final retort.

Porter died "without a whimper." The time was exactly 8:00 p.m. Folks said the entire affair was committed, tried, and executed all within one hour—and at no cost to the county!

A *Flume* reporter hastened to the scene, providing this ghoulish description:

> One of the hands had lost a thumb, an ear had been bitten off in some fight; the broken jawbone had bled profusely from the blow given by the Marshal's cane, and the blood had run over and besmeared the dirty, pallid features, while the neck had stretched to twice its natural length.

Mission accomplished for the vigilantes.

After Porter was hanged, there was the occasional town ruckus, but another murder was not committed for twenty-one years. In 1901, Edward Kimble shot and killed his former faro partner, William Shaw, in Kimble's saloon. Kimble was acquitted on the grounds of justifiable homicide because Shaw was a much larger man than Kimble.

Can the twenty-one-year hiatus of murders in Alma be attributed to William J. Porter's luckless night? Although there's no way of knowing, many residents that night would have said "yes." Soon after the lynching, the grateful townspeople gave Marshal Link a revolver with the inscription, "Presented to L.M. Link by the citizens of Alma, for his prompt and fearless performance of duty on March 22nd, 1880."

Link later moved to Utah where he opened a saloon in Castle Dale. He was killed on August 18, 1901, by two villainous brothers, Fred and Peter Mickel, who allegedly rode with Utah's notorious Robber's Roost gang. The two had come into Link's saloon to play cards and over-turned the table when they finished their hands. Link admonished them, and Fred stabbed him in the chest with a pocketknife.

Just as Link had arrived at Carmody's murder scene a minute too late, Marshal Acord of Emory County, Utah, stepped into Link's bar at the moment of the stabbing. He arrested Fred Mickel upon finding Link mortally wounded. There was immediate talk of lynch-ing Mickel, but he was taken to Salt Lake City for safekeeping, unlike Link's own brief prisoner of 1880.

THE MURDER AND LYNCHING SITE TODAY

Marsh & Mullen Saloon no longer exists. It may have burned down in one of several town fires over the years. Likewise, Alma no longer has a city jail. It was replaced by the county courthouse jail built in Fairplay in 1874. In 1880, Alma's jail was described as "a small building on the outskirts of the town."

A group of Alma miners ready to head to the mines with their burro packed with supplies. Mining was the area's primary industry. *Courtesy Park County Local History Archives Source: Ed & Nancy Bathke Collection, T.C. Miller Photo*

A view of Alma taken in the 1880s, from north of the town. *Courtesy Park County Local History Archives. Source: Ed & Nancy Bathke Collection. George Mellon photo.*

Chapter Thirty

FIRST NAME CHARLIE
1873

The little village of Dudley, near the base of Mount Bross, was only three months old in the summer of 1873. A forest fire started nearby and was heading in Alma's direction. Most able-bodied men were doing what little they could to control the flames. The familiar black sky, usually sparkling with millions of silvery dots, was now a smoky orange fog. Workers could hear the crackling pine from far away. Fairplay's business district would burn to the ground only a few months later. Alma's business district burned twice in later years.

Amidst the fire mayhem, Alma had a murder and a nasty one at that on the night of June 29, 1873.

Alma, founded in 1872, had its share of saloons, as did most if not all of the Rocky Mountain mining camps. This was not always a bad thing. The saloon served as a place for men to congregate and swap stories, have a meal, and loosen their tongues with few drinks. These social comforts were of vital importance on the Colorado frontier, but on this particular night, instead of comfort, the saloon served up a fight that ended in a killing.

One of Alma's early inhabitants was an old-timer named C.W. Ginnis, a regular at Kirkpatrick's, the local saloon. This favorite watering hole had an especially good draw on the night of the murder. By 10 p.m., patrons were feeling no pain. Why they weren't fighting the fire is not known.

Another local, known only as Charlie, also frequented the bar and had spent most of June 29 drinking. Upon entering Kirkpatrick's, he immediately started in on Ginnis in front of the old-timer's friends, Mr. Howell and George Broghan.

"You're a God-damn liar!" Charlie yelled to Ginnis. After enduring more cursing and insults, Ginnis had enough. He picked up his stool and raised it in a threatening manner.

"Leave me alone or I'll hit you," Ginnis warned.

"For God's sake, keep quiet, man," saloon keeper James S. Clark admonished Charlie, trying to keep order. Unfortunately, his words had little effect. Ginnis's two friends interjected themselves into the fray.

"You should not abuse an old man like Ginnis," Broghan said with some force.

"Why, Ginnis is one of the worst old men in the country!" Charlie slurred back, then threatened, "I have a revolver and I'll shoot you!"

Another tipsy gentleman, James Martin, flourished his own revolver.

"Put the gun away now!" Mr. Howell warned Martin. Martin complied. Charlie had already caused enough commotion, and the place sure didn't need any more.

Things returned to normal for a few minutes. Charlie then directed his coarse remarks to the other patrons—that is, when he wasn't staggering in and out of the business, obviously intoxicated. He was mean and surly. Around 10 p.m., Clark made a move to stop the nonsense. He walked over to the door and opened it, sternly told Charlie: "If you have a home, you had better go to it."

Charlie went out all right, but in a few minutes he hollered from the steps, "I'll shoot the God-damn son-of-a-bitch!" With that, the saloon patrons scrambled for safety and ducked for cover.

Here the story diverges. Some of the eleven witnesses said that Charlie came back in, walked up to Broghan and hit him hard in the face, possibly with a rock clenched in his fist. Others said that Broghan stepped outside, where the two began arguing and they came to blows and both fell down. Charlie got up and kicked Broghan hard, ran down the road. Martin also came out, revolver still in hand.

Bloody and bruised, Broghan went back into the saloon, where the men gasped at his appearance. George W. Dews retrieved a washbasin so Broghan could clean up. Broghan expressed fear that he would be shot if he went back outside.

By now it was around 11 p.m., and Clark and Ginnis were tired. They began preparing their beds on the saloon floor. It was common for men to sleep in saloons in fledgling towns and mining camps in the early West. As Clark turned down the last light, he reassured Broghan that he could now leave the saloon under the cover of darkness. Broghan went out and no more was heard.

In the morning, D. W. Fyffe, who lived near the saloon, stepped out into the brilliant sunshine and immediately spied blood on the road in front of his house. Tracing the trail, he ended up in front of Kirkpatrick's saloon. He continued and discovered a body in front of Currier's stable. A revolver was nearby. The deceased was none other than Charlie, whose throat had been slit.

A coroner's inquest was quickly convened to take testimony from the various witnesses, including J. L. Quiggle, who asserted he saw Broghan that same morning, whittling a stick with a blood-stained knife. "That is what did the work," Broghan confessed matter-of-factly to Quiggle.

As the suspect whittled away, Quiggle observed the three-inch knife blade had been broken off as well. "I stabbed the man in self-defense," continued Broghan, "and if I had to do it all over again in the same circumstances, I would." He explained that Charlie had hit him with something, and fearing for his life, he stabbed him.

Witness Sam S. Davidson corroborated the story, saying that Broghan told him after Charlie hit him in the mouth, he cut him with a knife, but didn't know how badly he was hurt. Broghan had to protect himself because Charlie had a hold of him and was pounding him. Broghan then showed the knife to Davidson, who noticed blood on the blade, but the suspect claimed he had no idea he had killed the man.

What was the verdict of the impaneled jury?

The said jurors upon their oath do say that they find that the said Charlie (surname unknown) came to his death from the effect of a wound inflicted upon his throat by a knife in the hands of George Broghan on the night of June the twenty-ninth, A.D. 1873.

The key word *feloniously* was omitted from the jurors' findings, however, implying that the killer was never indicted because the jury believed the stabbing was in self-defense.

THE MURDER SITE TODAY

Kirkpatrick's is long gone and the exact location is unknown. But the South Park Saloon, Alma's modern-day offering, is a good place to hang your hat for a while.

The Southern Ranches

Ranching in the South Park Basin, the large grassy plain that extends south of Fairplay, was a prominent enterprise in the 1800s, just as in the Northern Ranches section. Homesteading was popular from the inception of the Homestead Act of 1862 until after World War I, giving rise to large spreads. A newspaper reporter visited the area in 1883 and wrote a lengthy column entitled, "Ranch Ramblings," describing the size and productivity of the area and each rancher's specific property. Sam Hartsel's holdings warranted a town being named after him.

The main land features in the southern end of the county are Thirtynine Mile Mountain and Black Mountain. Currant Creek begins approximately five miles west of Thirtynine Mile Mountain and parallels Colorado State Highway 9. This part of the county was the site of a number of large cattle and sheep operations and also hay and potato farms. The little town of Kester thrived in the late 1890s, had its own post office and voting precinct, but the town has long since vanished.

Guffey, the largest town, was founded in 1895 and was initially called the Freshwater Mining District by Cripple Creek-area miners who came in to prospect. In May 1896, the post office was named Guffey after James McClurg Guffey, a local benevolent miner. The town is only six miles north of the Fremont County border. According to a *Fairplay Flume* article from October 1, 2008, which cites research and writings by geologist Steven Veatch, Guffey sits in an ancient volcanic basin where three volcanoes erupted 34 million years ago. In 1907, an iron meteorite weighing 682 pounds was found in the Guffey vicinity. Two years later, it was purchased by the American Museum of Natural History for $1,500 and is the largest meteor ever found in Colorado.

The Guffey area also had two soda springs, the Iron Spring and Yellow Soda Spring, from which the local residents drank until the 1930s, often using the water to make lemonade.

Trout Creek Pass on Highway 285, descending into Chaffee County, is included in this chapter because it is in the southern portion of the county. It straddles Park and Chaffee Counties on Highway 285 at an altitude of approximately 9,500 feet. The pass is between Fairplay and Buena Vista and wends through a scenic canyon. Information about the Midland Bike Trail Route System, an extensive array of biking paths, is posted at the top of the pass on the west side.

The view today from the top of Trout Creek Pass looking northeast. During Park County's thriving railroad era in the late 1800s, the Midland Railroad and the Denver, South Park & Pacific Railroad crossed paths at the top of Trout Creek Pass. The area is now the hub of the Midland Bike Trail Route System. *Courtesy Christie Wright*

Chapter Thirty-One

TRAGEDY on TROUT CREEK PASS
1894

David Morris was born in Scotland and immigrated to the United States at around the age of twenty-two. Described in the June 7, 1894, issue of the *Fairplay Flume* as "a man over six feet tall, of rather spare figure, 52 years of age and with nothing in the least vicious or criminal-looking about his face," he gave no indication the day before his crime that murder was on his mind.

Morris was a tie-chopper, or tie-hack, on the Midland Railroad. Although the track was originally laid in to Trout Creek Pass in late 1879, the ties often had to replaced. His job was to cut down trees large enough to yield several railroad ties, cut the ties with a broad axe, peel the bark, and then finish the ties so they could be used on the railroad bed.

Morris worked with another chopper named Mr. Shelton, age sixty-one—a back-breaking job for a man that age. After cutting ties for half a day on June 6, 1894, the two stopped at a nearby saloon. Under the influence of considerable amounts of liquor, they proceeded to the Hilltop camp, located at the top of Trout Creek Pass, to collect their monthly pay from supervisor W. O. Rawlings. The tie camp was a station on the South Park railroad at the point where it crossed the Colorado Midland near the top of the Pass.

Morris and Shelton left together to return to their cabin at the tie camp, four miles from the Hilltop camp. A few hours later, Morris returned, asserting he had killed his friend. The men in camp did not pay much attention to him at first, but his persistence soon created a stir, and a party was formed to go check on Shelton. Sure enough, "Shelton's dead body was found soaking in a pool of blood;

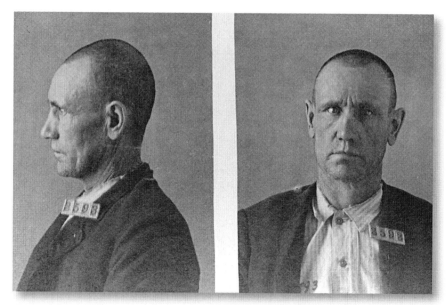

David Morris, sentenced to prison in October 1894 for stabbing his roommate to death. Morris was murdered two years after he was released from the territorial prison in Cañon City. *Courtesy Colorado State Archives.*

a big hole, two inches in depth, had been punched in the skull by some blunt instrument, and a dirk blade had pierced the heart," the *Buena Vista Herald* reported three days later.

The crime was assumed to have been committed on the Chaffee County side of the pass, and the undersheriff there was initially contacted. When it was determined the murder occurred on the Park County side, that county's sheriff was sent for. Sheriff Wilson and Deputies J. H. Fisher and C. S. Wells were preparing to escort convicted murderer Levi Streeter to the Colorado Territorial Prison in Cañon City to begin his sentence, so the foursome stopped long enough to pick up Morris on the way. The lawmen and Morris did not return to Fairplay until 10 o'clock that evening, and the suspect was promptly secured in the county jail. It was a long day's journey for all involved that had given Morris a firsthand look at where he would serve time if convicted.

The morning of June 7, a *Flume* reporter visited Morris in jail to get his version of the story. "What was the trouble between you and the dead man?" Morris was asked.

"There was none whatever," he replied. "We were good friends."

He admitted that he and Shelton stopped in a saloon and got drunk, but from that point he had no memory of any other events. "If it had not been for that hole (the saloon), this trouble would never have occurred!" he added bitterly. "But if I have committed this crime, I ought to suffer for it."

At the coroner's inquest held by Dr. Mayne on the night of the crime, the main witness was the driver of the tie-camp teams. Morris was confined until the next term of court, and on October 4, 1894, a jury found him guilty of second-degree murder. A week later, Judge Morton S. Bailey sentenced Morris to ten years in the penitentiary.

After serving four years in prison, Morris began his pardon requests. The first was scheduled for a hearing on August 5, 1898, along with hearings for fourteen other criminals. The hearing was rescheduled twice, and on October 8, his petition was refused. Undaunted, Morris waited and tried again, but his application did not come up until June 1, 1900; once again, he was denied for lack of evidence as to his innocence.

Morris apparently served out his sentence without receiving a pardon and upon his release, moved back to the Trout Creek Pass area. He continued working as a tie-hack and continued drinking.

On March 2, 1906, he was at a friend's house along with three other men, and all were imbibing. The homeowner, retired Major Isaac Taylor Withrow, and Morris had argued several days earlier in a saloon, but the point of contention is not known. In that argument, Morris threatened to stab Withrow. Now at Withrow's house, the conflict continued. It ended when Withrow took his rifle off the wall and shot Morris in the head. The three companions did not hear the rifle shot due to their drunken slumber and therefore were not called as witnesses. Withrow was convicted of second-degree murder in August 1906.

THE MURDER SITE TODAY

Trout Creek Pass on Highway 285, twenty-two miles south of Fairplay, has a pull-out in both the north and south directions. Caution is advised because of the traffic and a curve on the south side. A path on the north side leads to the bicycle trail signage and the site of the old railroad beds.

Allstrum homesteaded many acres near the convergence of Thirtyone Mile Creek and Currant Creek, along State Highway 9, north of Guffey. This photograph shows the general area where the homestead was located. No buildings are left. *Courtesy Christie Wright*

Chapter Thirty-Two

THOSE DELINQUENT HOGS
1884

P eter Allstrum was a well-known South Park homesteader
in the southern portion of Park County near Guffey, where
Thirtyone Mile Creek empties into Currant Creek. His 1888
homestead papers offer an interesting insight into the county's
ranching lifestyle during that era. His property included a one-story,
eighteen-by-thirty-foot log house with three rooms, three doors,
and windows, valued at $250. Household furniture included four
beds, one table, twelve chairs, stoves, cooking utensils, and an
organ. This was for himself, his wife, and their seven children.

Allstrum raised potatoes plus oats and wheat for cattle feed—he
grew ten thousand pounds of potatoes one year! Allstrum was also
the mail carrier for the Currant Creek area and postmaster for the
town of Kester. He contracted to carry the mail three times a week
between Cañon City and Hartsel, a distance of fifty-six miles one
way. He was of Swedish descent and had a stern look that usually
commanded respect.

Allstrum's wife, Christina, raised hogs for additional income.
The herd of swine had been "rooting up" the land belonging to a
neighbor, a young rancher and former teamster named Horace
Voss. Voss was described in the June 19, 1884, issue of the *Fairplay
Flume* as "a man of violent passion, fond of intemperate language
and had created serious trouble and nearly broken up two happy
homes in that neighborhood through his disregard of the marital
relation as applied to others."

On June 14, Voss accosted Allstrum on the road near their ranches
and demanded ten dollars for damages done to his property by Mrs.

Allstrum's hogs, or he would retaliate. Allstrum replied the hogs were his wife's. At that moment, Mrs. Allstrum came down the road, driving the delinquent hogs home. An animated argument ensued. Peter Allstrum ran home twice, first obtaining a pistol and the second time grabbing his rifle after Voss struck his wife in the face with a piece of fence rail. Voss had also gone home, returning on horseback and threatening to "bury the son-of-a-bitch there." When Voss dismounted and moved to throw a large rock at him, Allstrum fired, filling his neighbor full of lead. The newspaper reports did not mention that Allstrum's oldest daughter witnessed the entire affair and begged her father not to shoot.

Instead of tending to the wounded man, the Swede walked to his ranch house. In his wife's written statement to the coroner, she stated, "After Pete shot, he turned and walked toward home. When I got home, Pete told me he would leave to go and give himself up and started off horseback, without going in the house."

Allstrum loaded up some potatoes, hitched his team, and started out to find the justice of the peace on Currant Creek to give himself up. Finding none, he drove twenty-five miles into Garo and told Justice Edward Stephens of the shooting. The two then made the eleven-mile trip into Fairplay where, after a preliminary examination, Allstrum was placed on $5,000 bond by Justice John F. Smith. It was not known until the following day that Voss had died. His heart was pierced by Allstrum's one bullet.

A coroner's inquest was held at the defendant's home, with the stern warning on June 16, 1884, to those summoned to either appear or "answer the contrary at your Peril." The inquest members ruled the act a felonious killing. The ranchman's plea was self-defense.

The following month, the victim's father, John T. Voss, arrived in Park County from the Cripple Creek Mining District to investigate his son's murder. The senior Voss had retired in 1881 as an original member of the Crawford County, Kansas, Bar Association. He was known there as "a sledge-hammer lawyer, ever active, persistent, vigilant, in his client's interest, fighting in his behalf to the bitter end," according to the 1905 book, *A Twentieth Century History and Biographical Record of Crawford County, Kansas*, Voss was also part-owner of the Keystone Mining Company, which had nine

claims in the Cripple Creek District. There, he established himself as
a prosecuting attorney, presumably built on his Kansas reputation.

The *Fairplay Flume* newspaper of July 3, 1884, reported that
Voss "will make it his business to prosecute the case in hand to the
utmost." One can imagine how difficult it must have been to see
the site of his son's killing, with the Allstrum cabin nearby, when he
went to inspect the scene, knowing the murderer was free to return
home until his day in court.

The trial commenced almost one year after the shooting
and lasted a week. John T. Voss was one of the prosecutors. Mrs.
Allstrum, who was pregnant, stayed in town and was so distraught
at one point that she had to be led out of the courtroom by a friend.
A verdict of manslaughter was returned after only one night's delib-
eration but with a recommendation of mercy to trial Judge William
Harrison. After a motion for a new trial was denied, Allstrum was
sentenced to two years' hard labor. Sheriff Burns escorted Allstrum
to Cañon City forthwith.

The rancher fared satisfactorily in prison. A friend visited
him and reported back that he "looked well" and expected to be
released at the end of his time for good behavior. Christina raised
their many children and bravely managed the ranch by herself during her husband's absence. During his incarceration, she gave birth
to twins, Charles and Julia, expanding the family to nine children.

However, another turn of bad luck happened in February 1886
when all the ranch buildings burned down. Mrs. Allstrum broke her
arm and one of the team horses died. Because she was destitute,
her friends petitioned Governor Benjamin Eaton to grant clemency,
as did the trial judge, all Park County officers, the local justices
(including W. F. Bailey), and seven of the jurymen. A full pardon
was immediately granted to her husband.

Allstrum returned to southern Park County, leased a ranch in
Howbert in 1888, and sold cigars and liquor in the Howbert Saloon.
After doing some mining in the Pulver District near Wilkerson Pass,
the family moved on to Cripple Creek, where several of his sons
took up mining. Five family members are buried in the Mount
Pisgah Cemetery in Teller County, including Peter and "Christena
M.," his wife.

Peter Allstrum's mug shot, taken upon his arrival at the Colorado State Penitentiary. *Courtesy Colorado State Archives*

THE MURDER SITE TODAY

Allstrum's property was located at the confluence of Thirtyone Mile Creek and Currant Creek. No buildings are visible from the highway today, but the general area can be seen from State Highway 9, approximately one-half mile west of the turn-off for Guffey (County Road 102). If stopping, choose a safe pull-out along the highway and do not trespass on the private ranches in this area.

The Buffalo Slough area in the general vicinity of Fyffe's ranch. *Courtesy Christie Wright*

Chapter Thirty-Three

FEARLESS OBE FYFFE
1891

S even years after the Voss murder, another ranchman was shot and killed by his neighbor in southern Park County. Prominent sheep rancher Artemas C. Scribner was nephew to both Benjamin F. Spinney of Spinney Reservoir and Jerome E. Harrington, an attorney and highly regarded rancher.

Scribner's property was located next to an old-timer named Elias Obadiah "Obe" Fyffe, who had moved to the county in the 1870s. Fyffe's homestead was approximately five miles south of Hartsel in a remote area called Buffalo Slough.

By all accounts, Fyffe was a prosperous citizen. He had been a delegate to the Republican County caucus representing the Hartsel area. In January 1885, he had purchased a large spread called the Buffalo Slough Ranch, where he raised horses. He and his brother were part-owners of the Little Champion Mine on North Mosquito Mountain, a fairly good silver mine.

Fyffe and Scribner did not get along because Scribner "ran his sheep all over my ranch," according to Fyffe, even after he repeatedly told Scribner to stop. Fyffe raised cattle, and cattle did not mix well with sheep because of their different grazing habits. Scribner sent Fyffe several nasty letters in 1890 and teased him when he backed down from a fight.

On April 24, 1891, the day before the fatal confrontation, Scribner's sheepherder, C. H. Pickens, drove Scribner's flock onto Fyffe's property. Enraged, Fyffe told him to inform his employer that, if this continued, he would kill him. The next day, Fyffe and his wife, Eva May, were on horseback when they saw the herder coming onto their property. This time, Pickens had a gun and was accompanied by Scribner. "Keep outside the fence," Fyffe yelled, but the two ignored the warning and continued on. Grabbing his Winchester, Fyffe dismounted and pointed the gun at the neighbor while balancing the weapon on his horse's back. "Stand back!" he shouted, "or I will fill you so full of lead, the smelters will want you for what there is in you."

"You dirty cur, you don't dare to shoot," Scribner hollered back, and as he bent down to pick up a large stone to hurl at his neighbor, Fyffe shot him in the forehead from thirty feet away. Mrs. Fyffe screamed. Obe went to comfort her. Pickens dashed off to tell the victim's two uncles what had happened.

Fyffe then mounted and started the long twenty-five mile ride into Fairplay to turn himself in to avoid being lynched. Instead of taking the traveled roads, he hung back in the hills, uncertain as to how people in the area would react once the news reached them. By coincidence, he encountered the sheepherder's brother, John Pickens, and his wife while riding into town. Fearful of what John might do, Fyffe held a gun on him for a few minutes; however, John said there had been shooting enough and he would not harm Fyffe. Mrs. Pickens told him, "You'll get a rope around your neck for this."

Once Fyffe reached Fairplay, he was jailed and remained there until he requested bail on May 28.

A jury was selected on June 30, after the attorneys questioned sixty local citizens. Fyffe and his attorneys were not happy with the process because Fyffe was acquainted with only four of the men chosen, and his lawyer was not allowed to question them as to their character. Additionally, the court denied two continuances for Fyffe to locate several material witnesses who could testify about the victim's threats against the defendant.

The prosecuting attorney was Morton S. Bailey, a judge from the Cañon City area. He took two hours after lunch for his opening remarks. Bailey asserted the evidence would show Fyffe "used his horse as a breastwork, from behind which he shot Scribner with no warning."

Defense counsel was John G. Taylor, assisted by Vinton G. Holliday and a Mr. Horine. The trial lasted four days, from June 30 to July 3, 1891. Fyffe himself testified the entire day on July 2 and

seemed to impress the jury. The court allowed Fyffe's attorney
to introduce several threatening letters the victim wrote to the
suspect a year prior to the murder. Next up was herder Pickens who
stretched the court members to their very limits because he repeated
the entire scenario he witnessed instead of answering a single
question. The hearing could have been significantly shorter had it
not been for his labored style.

Pickens did offer some relevant information, but his version
conflicted with Fyffe's in three areas. First, Pickens testified that Eva
May came to the scene right after the shooting and therefore did
not witness the actual event, whereas Fyffe indicated his wife was
present the entire time. Secondly, Pickens estimated the victim
was shot from only "a rod away," or about sixteen feet, but Fyffe
claimed the distance was double that. Finally, Pickens asserted that
Fyffe uttered no warning before firing, whereas Fyffe indicated he
gave two warnings before firing. Pickens's most damaging testimony
was that when he called Fyffe a coward and accused him of being
afraid of Scribner, Fyffe had answered that "he was not afraid of him
and would kill him on sight the first time he got him alone."

Lastly, Eva May Fyffe was put under oath. She testified to
"having been in full view of the fatal scene and she substantiated
the evidence of her husband throughout."

Concluding the murder trial on the day before Independence
Day 1891 was a bad omen for Obe Fyffe. Charles A. Wilkin made
formidable closing remarks that went an hour longer than Bailey
had taken in his opening oration. The jury deliberated for eleven
hours, late into the night, and found the prisoner guilty of second-
degree murder. Although the jury recommended clemency in
sentencing, Judge Samuel P. Dale imposed an astonishing thirty
years in prison on July 7, 1891, after denying an appeal motion
filed after the verdict was rendered.

Fyffe applied for a pardon three years after the killing, coinci-
dentally along with another Park County murderer, Librado Mora,
on January 28, 1894, and ten others, to be heard on February 2,
1894. Either this hearing was continued or denied, for he submitted
a second application on March 13 to be heard on April 6. This time,
his request was mixed in with twenty-three others. Apparently this
was continued since he filed yet another petition to be heard on

May 4. The Board of Pardons ultimately refused to act in Fyffe's favor.

January 1895 saw the Park County inmate released on executive clemency in a surprise move by the new governor, Davis H. Waite, who also pardoned a murderer from Ouray County and several robbers. Part of the reason for Fyffe's release was that his mental health had been adversely affected by his confinement.

Fyffe seemed to have a particularly hard fall from grace after his conviction. Two years into his sentence, Eva May divorced him in March 1893 and remarried Oliver B. Hook in Glenwood Springs, Colorado. The judge signed the divorce decree and the marriage certificate almost simultaneously.

Secondly, gold was discovered in the middle of his ranch only eight months after the divorce, prompting the cry of "Buffalo Slough or Bust!" according to the *Flume* headlines of November 30, 1893. By this time, however, his ranch had fallen into the hands of a land company, and court proceedings were required to interpret the title transfer. He would not have reaped any profits. The new district was to be called Hartsel Gold Mining District, with claims fifteen hundred feet long by 300 feet wide. However, not much more was reported on the area, and it presumably played out quickly. Beyond these setbacks, Fyffe's lot in life after his release is unknown.

THE MURDER SITE TODAY

The Buffalo Slough area is located five miles south of Hartsel. Drive south a little over two miles from Hartsel on State Highway 9. Turn right onto County Road 53 and drive five miles. Fyffe's ranch was in this general area. This is private ranch land; please do not trespass. Pay attention to landmarks and return by the same route, as there are no services in this remote area of the county.

Obe Fyffe, who owned a horse ranch and several mines, had a particularly hard fall from grace after shooting his neighbor during an argument over property boundaries. *Colorado State Archives*

This photo of Guffey, circa 1900, shows a thriving town. *Courtesy Park County Local History Archives # 2596*

Chapter Thirty-Four

THE FALL of the FRESHWATER KING
1896

I n 1895, the area eighteen miles west of Cripple Creek was
known as the Freshwater Mining District. Business was booming
after Cripple Creek miners came into the area to escape labor
disputes. A "boomer", who presented himself as Charles T. Case,
popped up that September. Case was a mining camp promoter
whose real name was George M. Wright. He was good looking with
a suave demeanor and a melodic, mesmerizing voice, and he had
a list of aliases as long as his arm.

Case "boomed" four mining companies, the townsite itself, and
even a railroad company in his heyday in Guffey. He claimed to
own a bank building, a home, two office buildings, and vacant lots
in either Cripple Creek or Guffey. All this—and the way he spent
money—earned him the nickname "King of Freshwater." He was
well-liked and considered a good fellow.

One of Case's partners was Dr. William D. "Don" Crampton,
a feeble gentleman who lived on Currant Creek near Guffey; his
brother John C. Crampton lived nearby, and a young man named
John G. Sipchen lived with him. On January 16, 1896, Dr. Crampton
was murdered in what was deemed "one of the most atrocious
and terrible in its detail on record in Colorado." The poor man was
beaten, then shot once in the forehead and once on the right side
of the head. After death, the perpetrator fired more bullets into
the body and, in a final insult, hid the corpse under a manure pile.
There was evidence at the scene that the killers planned to burn the
body but were scared away before they made off with five dollars
and his valuables.

A search party was organized after Dr. Crampton went missing, and Case was one of the most active in the hunt. The party found the doctor's dog first. It had been shot in the head. On January 20, the body was discovered by John Crampton, who had received a tip from his friend, John F. Murray. Murray had seen three men in Dr. Crampton's cabin cooking dinner four days after he was killed. Two were local boys, Alfred and "Cal" Dell, but the third man, John G. Sipchen, was a newcomer and unknown in that country.

The coroner's jury was unable to come to any conclusion other than the victim had been killed by unknown parties. The jury foreman was none other than Case, and this was part of the reason no further conclusions were reached. Another jury member was Patrick Monaghan (frequently misspelled as Moynahan). The Park County Commissioners offered a $250 reward for the apprehension of the murderer or murderers, as did Governor Albert McIntyre on February 14.

Sheriff Wilson and his deputy, Mr. Smart, continued working the case as time allowed. One and a half years later, in September 1897, they arrested three men for the murder: John Sipchen, Patrick Monaghan, and James Day. It is unknown how the latter two figured in, as they were not the men seen at the victim's cabin with Sipchen on January 20, 1896. Case was also a suspect but had absconded back East to avoid arrest after information filed with the justice of the peace on August 25, 1897, named him as a codefendant.

Sipchen demanded a hearing in front of Guffey Justice of the Peace Gustave "Gus" Cohen, which was continued until September 15. The suspects were represented by Judge Holliday. The little courtroom was packed due to the high level of interest in the case. State's witnesses included old-time ranchers such as the Dells, Hammonds, Mr. Goodnight, and Mr. Smart. The hearing was continued to September 20, at which time the court bound over Sipchen for trial in District Court and set bail at $1,000. Sipchen arranged for bail and, on September 17, requested a continuance because of "important testimony which I have been unable to procure after due diligence." Codefendants Monaghan and Day were discharged without so much as a preliminary examination.

Sipchen had come west from Iron River, Michigan, where a Chicago, Illinois, newspaper described him as "always one of our

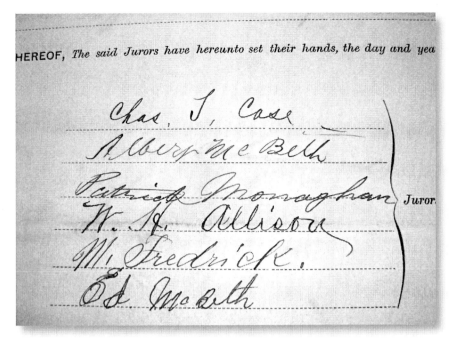

Con man George M. Wright, listed here as Chas. T. Case, purposely served on his own victim's jury to ward off suspicion on himself. *Courtesy Colorado State Archives*

most popular and respected young men." He attended Calvary College in Wisconsin and the Oshkosh Normal School. "His habits were always of the best and as far as we know, was never known to be under the influence of liquor," according to a quote in the October 22, 1897, issue of the *Flume* that came from the Chicago Record newspaper.

During the fall 1897 session of the District Court, charges against Sipchen were dismissed.

Charles Case, or George M. Wright, left an incredible trail of bewildering events that led lawmen on a chase throughout much of the country. Wright, as he will now be referred to, grew up in Michigan where he attended law school. Even before he married, he was dabbling in unscrupulous schemes, but he had never shown signs of being a murderer. A sheriff in Utah, who spent years tracking Wright to bring him to justice, came close to being Wright's undoing.

One year before Wright's arrival in Park County, three young men, all cousins, were killed at Pelican Point, Utah, just west of

Provo: Albert Enstrom, age twenty-two; Andrew Johnson, age twenty; and Alfred Nielson, age seventeen. The boys, who worked at the Hayes ranch, had been shot. Their bodies were loaded into a wagon along with all their possessions and driven by a team of horses onto the frozen Utah Lake. They were dumped into an icy grave through a hole cut in the ice. Two months later, in April 1895, a sheepherder found one of the bodies floating on the lake shore, and the two other bodies surfaced two days later.

Suspicion fell upon the ranch owner Harry F. Hayes because he acted "peculiarly" and because Albert Enstrom was his stepson, whom he did not treat well. He was indicted for the murders on December 4, 1896, and convicted on April 14, 1897. Death by hanging was the court's sentence, and his attorney appealed to the Utah Supreme Court, which delayed the sentence for nearly one year. His execution date was set for January 23, 1897. Another appeal was filed twenty days before sentencing but again denied, so the attorney filed with the Board of Pardons on the basis of insufficient evidence. Hayes's sentence was commuted to life in prison just two days before his scheduled execution.

Sheriff George A. Storrs spent several years investigating the offense. In his own words to the *Salt Lake City Tribune* on April 16, 1899: "I became very much interested in the case, owing to the fact that I had come so near to hanging Hayes. . . . I purchased some new rope at St. Louis with which to hang Hayes." Two years later, his exhaustive investigation revealed that Wright was the murderer. A pardon was filed on Harry Hayes's behalf, and his sentence was commuted to life in prison on January 16, 1897. A second petition was filed in April of 1899 by Sheriff Storrs, and Hayes was set free on May 6, 1899.

Wright was slippery, bobbing up in Indiana, then in San Francisco in 1902. Suddenly he was in Honolulu, New Jersey, West Virginia and many other states. It became almost a modern-day version of Elvis sightings. Law officers across the country who thought they saw him dutifully reported the incidents to Sheriff Storrs, who spent five years hunting the elusive con man and murderer. There is no conclusive evidence that Wright was ever apprehended.

One of two soda springs used by the town is still visible on the outskirts of Guffey, approximately one mile south of town. *Courtesy Christie Wright*

THE MURDER SITE TODAY

The Crampton homestead is on the left approximately twenty miles from Hartsel and five miles west of Guffey on State Highway 9. Dr. Crampton's homestead included two parcels along Currant Creek that can be seen from State Highway 9. Find a safe pull-out to stop and view the ranchland where a serial killer prowled so long ago. The land is privately owned and trespassing is prohibited.

❧ BIBLIOGRAPHY ❧

BOOKS

American Biographical History of Eminent and Self-Made Men, Volume 2, Western Biographical Publishing Co., 1878.

Anderson, Cynthia Peabody. *Pioneer Voices from to Breckenridge: The Peabody Family over Eleven Generations.* Breckenridge, Colorado: Alpenrose Press, 1999.

Bancroft Hubert Howe and Victor, Frances Fuller. *History of, and, 1540-1888,* Vol. XXV. San Francisco: The History Company, 1890.

Barth, Richard C. *Pioneers of the Colorado Parks: North, Middle and South Parks from 1850 to 1900.* Caldwell, Idaho: Caxton Printers, 1997.

Bjorklund, Linda. *Doin' Time in Fairplay.* Hartsel, Colorado: self-published, 2003.

Boessnecker, John. *Gold Dust and Gunsmoke.*: John Wiley & Sons, 1999.

Brown, Robert L. *Ghost Towns of the.* Caldwell, Idaho: Caxton Printers, 1973.

Brown, Robert L. *Ghost Towns of the.* Caldwell, Idaho: Caxton Printers, 1990.

Cleere, Jan. *Outlaw Tales of .* Guilford, Connecticut: Morris Book Publishing, 2006.

Cook, David J. *Hands Up.* Torrington, Wyoming: The Narrative Press, 2001.

Dallas, Sandra. *Colorado Ghost Towns and Mining Camps.* Norman: University of Oklahoma Press, 1988.

Enss, Chris. *Hearts West: True Stories of Mail Order Brides on the Frontier.* Helena, Montana: Twodot, 2005.

Epling, Phillip K. *"Bad John Wright:" The Law of Pine Mountain.* Prestonburg, Kentucky: Williams Press, 2009.

Fossett, Frank. *Colorado, Its Gold and Silver Mines, Farms and Stock Ranges, and Health and Pleasure Resorts, A Tourist's Guide.* New York: C.G. Crawford, 1880.

Gardiner, Harvey N. *Mining among the Clouds: The Mosquito Range and the Origins of 's Silver Boom.* Denver: Colorado Historical Society, 2002.

Griswold, Don, et al. *Colorado's Century of "Cities."* Denver, Colorado: Smith-Brooks, 1958.

Griswold, Don and Jean Harvey Griswold. *History of, Colorado, Vols. 1 and 2.* Colorado Historical Society in cooperation with the University of Colorado Press, 1996.

Hall, *A History of Colorado, Vol. IV.* Chicago: Blakely Printing Company, 1895.

Harrison, Fred. *Hell Holes and Hangings.* New York: Ballantine Books, 1968.

Henn, Roger. *Lies, Legends & Lore of the San Juans (and a Few True Tales).* Ouray, CO: Western Reflections Publishing, 1999.

Hill, Alice Polk. *Colorado Pioneers in Picture and Story.*: Brock-Haffner Press, 1915.

Home Authors. *A Twentieth Century History and Biographical Record of Crawford County, Kansas,* Chicago: Lewis Publishing Company, 1905.

Jessen, Kenneth. *Colorado Gunsmoke.* Boulder, Colorado: Pruett Publishing, 1986.

Judd, Deacon. *Nuggets from Park County, Colorado.* Fairplay, Colorado: self-published, 1987.

Leonard, Stephen J. *Lynching in Colorado 1859–1919.* Boulder: University of Colorado Press, 2002.

Lohse, Joyce B. *First Governor, First Lady, John and Eliza Routt of Colorado.* Palmer Lake, Colorado: Filter Press, LLC, 2002.

Mather, Ruth E. and Fred C. Boswell. *Gold Cap Desperados.*: University of Oklahoma Press, 2000.

Murphy, Jan. *Outlaw Tales of : True Stories of 's Robbers, Rustlers and Bandits.* Guilford, Connecticut: Globe Pequot Press, 2006.

McGrath, Maria Davies. *The Real Pioneers of Colorado.*: The, 1934, Document Division of the Denver Museum, CWA Project 51.

Parson, Eugene. *A Guidebook to Colorado.*: Little, Brown and Company, 1911.

Portrait & Biographical Record of the State of Colorado.: Chapman Publishing Company, 1899.

Portrait and Biographical Record of Denver and Vicinity, Colorado: containing portraits and biographies of many well known citizens of the past and present, together with biographies and portraits of all the presidents of the United States. Denver: Chapman Publishing Co, 1898.

Pretti, Roger. *Mining, Mayhem and other Carbonate Excitements.* Vail, Colorado: Vail Daily Press. 2003.

Price, Charles F. *Season of Terror: The Espinosas in Central Colorado, March–October 1863.* Boulder: University of Colorado Press, 2013.

Representative Men of Colorado. Denver, Colorado: Rowell Art Publishers, 1902.

Robinson, T.M. Reporter. *The Decisions of the Court of Appeals of the State of Colorado, Including Cases Determined at the April and September Terms, 1894, and the January Term 1805.* Vol. 5, Albany, New York: Banks & Brothers Law Publishers, 1896.

Simmons, Virginia McConnell, *Bayou Salado.* Colorado Springs, Colorado: Century One Press, 1996.

Smiley, Jerome, *History of Denver.* Denver, Colorado: *The Denver Times,* Times Sun Publishing Company, 1901.

Smith, Duane. *Horace Tabor: His Life and the Legend.* Boulder: University of Colorado Press, 1989.

Smith, Duane. *Rocky Mountain Mining Camps.* Lincoln: University of Nebraska Press, 1967.

Stone, Wilbur F. *History of Colorado, Vol. I.* Chicago: S.J. Clarke Publishing Company, 1919.

Thrapp, Dan L. *Encyclopedia of Frontier Biography, Volume 1: A-F.* Lincoln: University of Nebraska Press, 1991.

Ubbelohde, Carl, Maxine Benson, and Duane A. Smith. *A Colorado History.* Colorado: Pruett Press, 1965.

Vickers, William B. *History of the City of Denver, Arapahoe County, and Colorado: Containing a History of the State of Colorado . . . a condensed sketch of Arapahoe County . . . a history of the city of Denver . . . biographical sketches.* O.L. Baskin & Co., 1880.

Wilson, Michael R. *Frontier Justice in the Wild West: Bungled, Bizarre, and Fascinating Executions.* Guilford, CT: Globe Pequot Press, 2007.

Wommack, Linda: *From the Grave: A Roadside Guide to Colorado's Pioneer Cemeteries.* Caldwell, Idaho: Caxton Press, 1998.

DOCUMENTS and PERIODICALS

Adkins, Tony. "Letter on Dolph Draughan." *The Appalachian Quarterly,* (Sept. 2003): 39.

Col. Jairus Hall, articles and photos donated by descendant William Clark, Local History Archives, Bailey, Colorado.

Coroner Reports (originals and copies), Park County Local History Archives. "The Daniel's Hill Fight." *Geocities.com.* www.geocities.com/Athens/Delphi/2839/daniels.html (Jan. 6, 2000).

District Court trial transcripts, Benjamin Ratcliffe trial, Park County Local History Archives, Bailey, Colorado.

District Court trial transcripts, Dr. Joseph Condon trial, Park County Local History Archives, Bailey, Colorado.

District Court records and dockets book, 1881 – 1896, Park County District Court, Fairplay, Colorado.

Inventory of Park County records, Colorado State Archives, Denver, Colorado.

Luntz, Ben. "Special Focus: Dolph Draughan, Talt Hall, Calib Jones, Devil John Wright and Their Feuds." *The Appalachian Quarterly,* (June 2003): 4-25.

Michal, Edward J., *Charles Lewis Hepburn: An Early Entrepreneur.* Transcript of unpublished diary, Park County Local History Archives, Bailey, Colorado.

Minke, Gary. "Puma City Murder." Proceedings of the South Park Symposium. Fairplay Colorado, 2004.

"Park County Statistics," South Park Chamber of Commerce, Park County, Colorado. September 3, 2007.

Personal diary, May – October, 1870 by Mrs. Charles Hepburn, transcribed by Edward J. Michal. Park County Local History Archives, Bailey, Colorado.

United States Department of Agriculture. "2007 Census of Agriculture," Park County, Colorado.

NEWSPAPERS

Relevant issues from 1860 to 1926

Akron Weekly Pioneer Press, Akron, Colorado

Aspen Tribune, Aspen, Colorado

Breckenridge Bulletin, Breckenridge, Colorado

Carbonate Chronicle, Leadville, Colorado

Carroll Daily Sentinel, Carroll, Iowa

Chicago Daily Tribune, Chicago, Illinois

Daily Miner Register, Central City, Colorado

Daily Register-Call, Central City, Colorado

Daily Gazette, Colorado Springs, Colorado

Daily Tribune, Salt Lake City, Utah

Denver Post, Denver, Colorado

Denver Evening Post, Denver, Colorado

Denver Weekly Commonwealth, Denver, Colorado

Des Moines Daily Reader, Des Moines, Iowa

Fairplay Flume, Fairplay, Colorado

Gazette Telegraph, Colorado Springs, Colorado

Georgetown Courier, Georgetown, Colorado

Hazel Green Herald, Wolfe County, Kentucky

Janesville Gazette, Janesville, Wisconsin

Leadville Chronicle, Leadville, Colorado

Leadville Daily Herald, Leadville, Colorado

Leadville Weekly Herald, Leadville, Colorado

Licking Valley Courier, West Liberty, Kentucky

Logansport Pharos, Logansport, Indiana

Montezuma Millrun, Montezuma (Summit County), Colorado

Morning Herald, Lexington, Kentucky

New York Times, New York, New York

Park County Bulletin, Alma, Colorado

Rocky Mountain News, Denver, Colorado

Saguache Chronicle, Saguache, Colorado

Salt Lake Tribune, Salt Lake City, Utah

Semi-Weekly Tribune, Salt Lake City, Utah

Summit County Journal, Summit County, Colorado

Weekly Register-Call, Central City, Colorado

WEB SITES

Barnes, Shelley and Carpenter, Tina. "Como Cemetery." *Colorado GenWeb Project.* http://files.usgwarchives.org/co/park/cemeteries/como.txt.

Culver, Joyce Escue. "Uplide Vallie." *Find A Grave Memorial # 32883906.* www.FindAGrave.com.

Love, Margaret Cole. ": Automatic Restoration of Rights." *Relief from the Collateral Consequences of Criminal Conviction.* April, 2007.

www.sentencingproject.org/doc/File/Collateral%20Consequences/Colorado. pdf

Public Member Family Trees for John Doolittle, Amos Brazille and Ella Vallie. www.ancestry.com

"Park County, Colo. Alma Cemetery." www.colorado gravestones.org.

"Park County Heritage." www.parkcoheritage.com

"South Park National Heritage Area," www.southparkheritage.org.

MAPS

State of Colorado. Colorado State Archives Corrections Records, Penitentiary Photograph Records, 1893-1980 and Record of Convicts (CD-ROM). Photo. . 1893-1980.

Chamberlain, W. G. "Mining Scene on Hoosier Pass" Photo. www.mining-bureau.com.

Connecting sheet. *Section 14 Township 6S Range 76W.* Map. U.S. Bureau of Land Management.

Montezuma Quadrangle. "Map of Old Webster Pass and Handcart Gulch." 1902.

⊰ACKNOWLEDGMENTS⊱

Thanks to my extended family who introduced me to Colorado history years ago and to my Loveland-area family, who have supported and encouraged me throughout the book's entire process and believed in my ability to bring it to completion.

Many thanks go my author and genealogy friends who patiently listened and offered excellent suggestions: Joyce Lohse, Kristine Wolberg, and Diana Copsey-Adams. I am indebted to author Charles F. Price for generously sharing his knowledge of the Espinosa brothers. Also to my many friends in Colorado Springs, the Denver area, and Park County who encouraged me along the way.

I thank History Colorado Curator Alisa Zahller, who provided my initial publishing opportunities in newspaper media.

Loveland photographer Sean Brubaker of Evoke Images deserves a personal thank-you for his endless patience and ability to capture the feeling.

Miners Dale Herbertson, Kenn Hicks, Maury Reiber, and the late Kevin Lawrence showed interest in the book throughout and taught me Colorado's mining history first-hand.

Thanks to Kenn Hicks and Donald Lamping for their insights into Riceville, the murder site in Chapter 1.

I appreciate the help of four descendants of the Draughn family—Rita Day, Debra Castro, Daniel Miller, and Tony Adkins—who provided family photos and documents for Chapter 7 and assisted me with the family's intricate genealogy.

Thanks to Chris O. Andrew, Grant Ralston, and Wendy Stelle for providing detailed family information for Chapter 14 on their ancestor, Benjamin Ratcliff, and for inviting me to the 2010 Ratcliff reunion in Park County.

Thanks to Robert Cornog and his family for sharing personal documents and photos of their ancestor, Gus Cornog, for Chapter 21. And, to Bill Clark and Jack Boot, thanks for sharing documents and photographs related to the Jairus W. Hall and Cassius Hall families in Section Two, Hall Valley.

Erik and Beth Swanson, long-time Alma residents, helped by sharing their extensive knowledge of the area's history, especially the Alma/Buckskin cemetery.

Thanks to the Park County Local History Archives board members who listened as I regaled them with tales of dastardly deeds during the research and writing stages of this book. Other Park County agencies also assisted: My thanks to the South Park Historical Foundation, Park County Historical Society and Friends of the various Park County Public Libraries. The South Park National Heritage Area staff provided guidance that is most appreciated. Thank you to Linda Balough and Erica Duvic, as well as Amy Unger, County Preservation Planner.

Thanks to Steve Plutt, resident historian of the Lake George/ Tarryall area, for sharing his knowledge of area history and cemeteries. Bob Schoppe and Tom Klinger of the Denver, South Park & Pacific Historical Society are also to be thanked for their invaluable help. I thank Bernie and Linda Nagy, who offered valuable advice on marketing and with whom I share a love of historic Park County photographs.

Colorado State Archives employees were a great help in allowing me to sort through boxes of court files and provided the priceless mug shots. Terry Ketelsen, Colorado State Archivist (now retired), offered much assistance during the research stage of the book.

Other helpful organizations include Women Writing the West and the Wild West History Association.

Thanks, too, to Doris and Tom Baker of Filter Press for believing in the value of the stories that lie within.

✣ABOUT the AUTHOR✣

Christie Wright is a Colorado "semi-native," who moved to the state after graduating from college in Illinois. After many adventures exploring the high country, she became fascinated with Park County mining camps and later expanded her interest to the county's overall history.

Christie worked as a state probation officer in Colorado Springs, Colorado, for more than twenty-two years and has applied her knowledge of Colorado's criminal court system to the historic murder stories in this book.

Christie currently serves as president of the Park County Local History Archives and is a member of Women Writing the West and the Wild West History Association. Her previous publications include *All That Lies Beneath*, a history of the Alma/Buckskin cemetery; articles in Park County's *Fairplay Flume* newspaper; and a geology article, co-authored with Steven W. Veatch, published in *New Mexico Geology*.

The author has lived in the Denver area since 2004.